Young People and the

Curse of Ordinariness

by the same author

Young People in Love and in Hate
ISBN 978 1 84905 055 5

Feeling Like Crap
Young People and the Meaning of Self-Esteem
ISBN 978 1 84310 682 1

Working with Anger and Young People
ISBN 978 1 84310 466 7

Listening to Young People in School, Youth Work and Counselling
ISBN 978 1 85302 909 7

Young People and the Curse of Ordinariness

Nick Luxmoore

Jessica Kingsley *Publishers*
London and Philadelphia

Extract from 'Selva Oscura' (MacNeice 1964) on p.6 is reproduced with permission from Faber & Faber.

Extract from 'Born Yesterday' (Larkin 1955) on p.16 is reproduced with permission from Marvell Press.

Extract from *A Return to Love* (Williamson 1992) on p.72 is reproduced with permission from HarperCollins.

'The Road Not Taken' (Frost 1920/2001) on p.82 is reproduced with permission from Random House Ltd.

Extracts from 'In Dreams Begin Responsibilities' (Schwartz 2003) on p.92 are reproduced with permission from Robert Phillips.

First published in 2011
by Jessica Kingsley Publishers
116 Pentonville Road
London N1 9JB, UK
and
400 Market Street, Suite 400
Philadelphia, PA 19106, USA

www.jkp.com

Library of Congress Cataloging in Publication Data
Luxmoore, Nick, 1956-
 Young people and the curse of ordinariness / Nick Luxmoore.
   p. cm.
 Includes bibliographical references.
 ISBN 978-1-84905-185-9 (alk. paper)
 1. Self-perception. 2. Group identity. I. Title.
 BF697.5.S43L896 2011
 155.5--dc22
                                  2010030008

British Library Cataloguing in Publication Data
A CIP catalogue record for this book is available from the British Library

ISBN 978 1 84905 185 9

Printed and bound in Great Britain by
MPG Books Group

For Debbie

'A life can be haunted by what it never was
If that were merely glimpsed.'

Louis MacNeice, 'Selva Oscura'

Contents

Acknowledgements

I'm grateful to Faber & Faber for permission to quote from Louis MacNeice's 'Selva Oscura' from *Selected Poems of Louis MacNeice*; to Marvell Press for permission to quote from Philip Larkin's 'Born Yesterday' from *The Less Deceived*; to HarperCollins Publishers for permission to quote from *A Return to Love* by Marianne Williamson © 1992 by Marianne Williamson, portions reprinted from *A Course in Miracles* © 1975 by Foundation for Inner Peace, Inc.; to The Random House Group Ltd. for permission to quote from 'The Road Not Taken' from *The Poetry of Robert Frost*, edited by Edward Connery Lathem, published by Jonathan Cape; and to Robert Phillips for permission to quote from Delmore Schwartz's short story 'In Dreams Begin Responsibilities' from *In Dreams Begin Responsibilities and Other Stories*.

I'm also grateful to colleagues at King Alfred's College, Wantage, for supporting my work, especially to Nick Young, Adam Arnell, Kate Baker and Diane Jones. I'm grateful to my supervisor, Jane Campbell, and to Kathy Peto, Debbie Lee, Chris Mowles and Jane Campbell for reading and commenting on drafts of this book. Lastly and most importantly, I'm grateful to Kathy, Frances and Julia.

Introduction

Again and again, young people return to the question, 'Am I the same as other people or am I different?' It's a hard question to answer. Everyone knows that they're the same as other people in lots of ways yet they suspect that they might also be different. Or they want to be different... Or they accuse other people of being different... Or they get beaten up for being different...

This book is about young people trying to find answers, or at least trying to live more comfortably with the question.

It's a question which affects everybody but adults usually get better at balancing sameness and difference as they get older, recognising that they're the same as other people in some ways and different from them in other ways. As adults, we may have our eccentricities and we may have done all sorts of strange things in our lives, but we're really no different from other people: in fact, we're *ordinary*. Growing older, we get better at accepting and balancing our particular limitations against the things that we can do and that we're good at doing. Yet this balancing is still disturbed from time to time by events in our lives and we get anxious all over again, worrying that we should be more of this or less of that.

Young people are forever struggling to find any sort of balance and, as a result, their anxiety about ordinariness affects everything: their behaviour, their choices, their relationships, their happiness. Lewis, for example, could never be ordinarily drunk like his friends: he had to be the *most* drunk; and so it was Lewis who nearly drowned after falling into the river. Holly couldn't just have sex with her boyfriend: she had to be the first of her friends to get pregnant. For some young people, ordinariness feels like a curse from which they must escape, and yet there are other young people desperate to be like everyone else. Majid settled for a B grade in Maths because getting an A would have marked him out and meant getting teased. Rosa decided not to compete in the swimming championships because none of her friends were particularly interested in swimming and they were all planning a sleepover that weekend.

Anxieties about ordinariness are at the heart of growing up and are expressed in all sorts of ways. As a school counsellor, I hear about things which happened at home last night and in town at the weekend. Sometimes young people are describing moments of surprise and connection, 'I used to think he was a complete idiot but he's all right really once you get to know him... Me and my mum had a talk and it's better now... We were sitting next to each other and it turns out that we both like the same things...' and sometimes they're alarmed by the disconnections they experience, 'I really hate the way they act when they're together... She's got no idea what I feel... I don't understand why he thinks it's funny...' They bring to counselling a continuing conversation with themselves about sameness and difference and a continuing attempt to find some sort of balance.

Like other professionals, my job is to help with this balancing so that young people can work hard, enjoy their lives and achieve all sorts of things without losing sight of the fact that – underneath everything and like everyone else – they're ordinary and there's nothing wrong with that: they don't have to be determinedly different from other people any more than they have to copy other people. But because sameness and difference exist in dynamic relationship to one another (Bateson 1979), the balance always tipping this way and that, young people like Lewis, Holly, Majid and Rosa can never be sure of their ground, always asking obliquely through their words or through their behaviour, 'Am I the same as other people or am I different? Am I normal?' If they can be helped towards answers or – more usually – towards a greater ability to tolerate *not knowing* the answers, then their anxieties about ordinariness are less likely to be enacted at their own or at other people's expense.

Not knowing whether we're like other people is difficult, however. Fourteen-year-old Ellis hates his life. 'It's so boring!' he says. 'Nothing ever happens! No one ever *does* anything!' What he means is that no one ever notices or seems to care. He feels as if he's just another name on the register, invisible and unimportant. So one morning he stomps into school, swears at a teacher and, by getting himself into trouble, finally gets himself some attention. From our conversations, it becomes clear that he has no idea whether other people sometimes feel the way he does or whether it's just him.

This book shares his anxiety about ordinariness and his need for attention. A book called *Young People and the Curse of Ordinariness* sounds like a Harry Potter story or like a computer game in which exciting things are bound to happen at any moment. It sounds like a story in which young people escape to other worlds, leaving behind all the frustrations and predictabilities of their ordinary lives. It doesn't sound like a book about everyday, mundane, repetitive interactions; about Ellis waking up in the same room in the same house with the same day stretching ahead and wondering, 'Is this normal? Is this how it's meant to be?' It's not a book called *Young People and the Problem of Living an Ordinary Life* but that's what it's about, really. Just as Ellis needs attention, this book needs its Harry Potteresque title to get attention because, by itself, ordinariness gets no one's attention, whether you're a young person or a book. That's the point. That's the anxiety.

When I see him a few days after the swearing-at-a-teacher incident, he's downcast. I ask how the last week has been and he complains that nothing's happened, 'As usual! Nothing ever happens!'

I could ask what he'd like to happen, but he wouldn't know. If I pushed him, he'd probably say that he'd like to be a *bit* different from other people but not too different; he'd like things to be more exciting (his motorbike is broken and he hasn't got the money to fix it); he'd like to be playing football right now or smoking a nice fat joint; he'd like to be a PE teacher; he'd *definitely* like to win the lottery; he'd like to be famous, going to amazing parties and flirting with amazing girls; he'd like to have people ringing him up, wanting to know what he's doing tonight, wanting *him*.

But none of these things is about to happen and so life feels boring, as if he's missing out, as if he's not interesting enough (see Chapter 4). From time to time he doubts my interest in him ('You only do this because it's your job!'), misses an appointment and, when we do meet again, hurls fresh despair at me, insisting that he should be more of this and less of that – more popular! more rich! more important! less criticised! less taken for granted! less bored! He swears and swears and swears.

I have no answers, but we keep on meeting, wondering together about the world he experiences and the world he'd *like* to experience. He's tortured by this imagined world (see Chapter 11), longing for it at the same time as he despises it for apparently excluding him, never sure whether his own experience with its ups and downs is a matter of good or bad luck or whether it's a mixture, a kind of ordinariness. 'Why can't anything good ever happen?' he says. 'It's the same crap every day. Every day! It's like I'm supposed to have done something wrong!'

So how do young people like Ellis live ordinary lives without feeling diminished? How can they be noticeable and important in their own ways without having to become recklessly self-destructive? How can they live with the apparent curse of ordinariness?

For young people there are competing voices. One goes, 'Why am I so boring, so ordinary? What did I do to deserve this? Why can't I be more popular, talented, attractive, intelligent? What did other people do to deserve all their luck, their happy families? Why can't I have those things?' With this voice nagging away inside, there are young people who long to be different in some way, in *any* way. But there's another voice they know equally well. It goes, 'Why am I different from other people? What's wrong with me? Why am I the weird one? Why is my skin, my accent, my sexuality, my way of doing things different from other people?'

With this voice uppermost, there are young people who long to fit in and grow to hate difference in any shape or form (see Chapter 2).

I think all young people hesitate somewhere on a continuum between these two voices, always trying to interpret their experience in relation to that of other people. Is this normal? Is this understandable? Do other people think and feel this way? If my experience is a *bit* like other people's and a *bit* different, then how exactly? And why? And is that okay? One of the many tasks of growing up is to find a way of approaching everyday life with enough certainty to feel safe and enough uncertainty to remain curious. We don't want all our days to be the same ('This is so boring!'), but nor do we want to live permanently on edge, never knowing what to expect ('This is so stressful!').

As Chapter 3 describes, our anxiety about this goes back to the beginning of our lives and our need to be recognised by a mother or mothering-figure. If that person doesn't recognise her baby, then the baby's life is potentially in danger. As babies, we therefore have to make ourselves familiar enough to be recognisable and yet different enough to stand out from all the other babies. I think we spend the rest of our lives wrestling with this paradox. Certainly, by the time they're thirteen, fourteen, fifteen or sixteen, young people again find themselves in the middle of another developmental transition where sameness and difference are major sources of anxiety. Being the same as other people sounds safe but also sounds boring; being different from other people sounds exciting but also sounds scary.

Ellis can't get it right. 'I just want to *be someone!*' he complains. For him, 'being someone' means being recognised as special, talented, unusual in some way, whereas being unrecognised means being a 'complete nobody'. Like babies, young people are always on the lookout for ways of being recognised whenever the threat of invisibility or of being a 'complete nobody' is greatest. Adam's way of 'being someone' was to beat up anyone who threatened his position as gang leader. Naima's way was to become indispensable as the person who listened to all her friends' problems. Biggi's way was to become a reliable source of cheap drugs. In another context, these behaviours might be thought of as finding a talent or finding a niche. It's just that these talents and these niches aren't always happy ones for the protagonists or for the people surrounding them. So this book is about helping young people to 'be someone' without having to become someone they're not.

Ordinariness gets a bad press. It's hard to write about someone being ordinary without having to rescue the word from associations with mediocrity and failure. In the UK, 'ordinary' is linked with 'common' which can be strongly pejorative, suggesting something dirty, promiscuous, inferior, worthless... Philip Larkin's (1955) poem 'Born Yesterday' departs from the norm. Instead of wishing all the usual things such as beauty, innocence and love for his friend's new-born daughter, Larkin wishes that she may grow up to be 'ordinary' without the bother of all those things to unbalance her life:

> In fact, may you be dull –
> If that's what a skilled,
> Vigilant, flexible,
> Unemphasised, enthralled
> Catching of happiness is called.

Larkin's wish for the baby is refreshing because so many young people grow up believing that happiness is to be found only in being extraordinary, exceptional, different from other people and so recognised at last. It's as if they're forever chasing the attention of some unreliable mother they've been carrying around in their heads, always believing that they must be more than they are because being ordinary won't do, being ordinary will never get her attention.

Part of my job is to help them understand that ordinariness is inevitable; ordinariness is a blessing rather than a curse. In saying that, I'm not suggesting that young people should settle for mediocrity, under-achievement or for a status quo in which disadvantaged young people are unable to escape their socio-economic origins. But there's an ideology which tries to oppose the survival-of-the-fittest, cream-always-rises-to-the-top, some-people-have-got-it-and-some-haven't tyrannies of capitalism by insisting that, on the contrary, given a fair start, everyone is capable of everything. I think this creates its own kind of tyranny. Young people hear this well-intentioned rhetoric from enthusiastic teachers and politicians and wonder why they can't seem to achieve all the amazing things expected of them. The pressure to be exceptional only complicates an abiding and much deeper struggle with the question, 'Am I the same as other people or am I different?' Because of the rhetoric of aspiration! aspiration! frantically directed at young people, I sometimes wonder whether we end up educating young people to be *dis*contented and whether, as a result, they end up like Ellis, always feeling that there's something missing from their lives, as if they're never good enough because they're ordinary people living in ordinary houses and doing ordinary jobs. When they hear from teachers and politicians about a world in which everything supposedly comes to those who want it badly enough (see Chapter 5), some panic: they set out to achieve impossible things, and when they can't achieve socially acceptable things, they set out to be exceptional in other ways by becoming the loudest, rudest, most aggressive, most lavish or most anti-social person around because, at least that way, they get to 'be someone'. No one says to them that, in fact, ordinariness is fine; ordinariness is the glue that holds society together; ordinariness is what we have in common and, in the face of death, it'll be our ordinariness which comforts and binds us together (see Chapter 8).

But for any counsellor, teacher, youth worker, social worker or parent trying to support young people who are struggling with all this, there's a dilemma... How far are we encouraging young people to be different from everyone else and how far are we encouraging them to be the same, to conform? Are we trying to change the world or keep it as it is? Involving ourselves with young people inevitably means remembering our own adolescence and (usually) our own sense of unfulfilled potential (Luxmoore 2008). We have our own ambivalent feelings about being ordinary (see Afterword). The danger is that we therefore interpret young people's best achievements as proof of their *extraordinariness* – an extraordinariness we've nurtured and can take pride in, as if we've finally proved something to ourselves about our own extraordinary capabilities.

I remember going to one school's prize giving. It was an autumn evening. The big assembly hall was decorated with flowers and buzzing with parents, grandparents and children too young to be left at home. In school uniforms, their older brothers and sisters sat near the stage, some tall, some small, some fat, some thin, some confident, some shy: a mixture of young people waiting to be celebrated for their academic progress, for their contributions to the community and for all the other things they'd achieved during the year.

The lights dimmed. With photographs of particular school events projected onto large screens behind, a few students told the story of the school year with its special occasions, exciting achievements and occasional mishaps. We clapped. The deserving students then stood and were called to the stage to receive their certificates. We clapped them all – one by one – and they seemed pleased. A few musical performances followed and the local dignitary who was presenting the certificates made a short speech.

There was just one award left to make, advertised in the programme as 'The Headteacher's Personal Award'.

She rose from her chair at the side of the stage and began to speak about 'this student'. Whoever he was, he'd evidently got top grades in all his exams, starred in all the recent school productions, captained umpteen sports teams, been on school trips around the world and single-handedly raised vast amounts of money for charity. To cap it all, he was now off to read Law at a prestigious university. Pictures of the demi-god in action flashed onto the screens behind and the headteacher paused to allow video clips of his various theatrical performances to be shown.

We were clapping intermittently but by now the atmosphere in the hall had collapsed. People were starting to fidget. I felt myself becoming more and more cynical and heard teachers behind me joking about not being fit to shake the student's hand. Yet still the eulogy continued until finally it was time for the young man to go onto the stage. We were doing our best to keep clapping but by now no one was interested. The prize-winning students in their uniforms looked thoroughly deflated, their parents anxious to get home.

Celebrations and prize givings like this one are important and there was so much about this one that was good: it was inclusive, warm-hearted and proportionate. Until the end! I know that headteachers are obliged to use the achievements of top students to advertise their schools. The problem was that in eulogising this particular student the headteacher managed to leave the rest of us feeling debilitated, wondering how on earth we could ever be as deserving as this extraordinary human being who'd clearly gone way beyond what the rest of us would ever be capable of achieving. Our own small accomplishments were as nothing compared to his remarkable feats.

Perhaps she simply misjudged the occasion. But I think her inclination to eulogise is typical of a rhetoric intended to inspire but which is actually more likely to dishearten. Like anyone, I believe in praising and rewarding young people wherever possible, noticing and applauding whenever good things happen. What's damaging is the implication (see Chapter 5) that we can and should be more than we are; the suggestion that we're all extraordinarily talented and that, if only we try hard enough, we can all be like 'this student', stepping onto the stage to receive our reluctant, ambivalent applause.

Everything that young people do is about getting used to the ordinary, unglamorous realities of life, learning to tolerate frustration and sometimes failure. Understandably, schools focus on success and on what will happen to young people as a result of success. They don't (or daren't) prepare young people for failure or for the degrees of failure which will inevitably be most people's experience. Consequently, I find myself forever meeting with young people who are grappling with what they experience as failure of one sort or another because, for them, anything that isn't outright success comes to seem like failure. It's as if there's nothing in between, no balancing, no sense of life being an ordinary mixture of things that go well and things that go badly. Apart from anxieties about academic failure, they bring to counselling all sorts of other perceived failures where life hasn't gone according to plan: failure to stop my dad hitting my mum, failure to be as good as my sister, failure to deal with the bullies, failure to keep my temper, failure to stop my brother's asthma attack, failure to say what I think, failure to keep my boyfriend for myself, failure to stop my mum drinking, failure to be the person everyone expects me to be…

This sense of personal failure is hard for young people to bear because it's so different from the way things were supposed to be. On the one hand, there's the world of limitless opportunity and success proposed by schools while, on the other, there's a residual sense of the world as it once was (probably before they emerged into it) and perhaps still could be (see Chapter 11). We never seem to lose our sense of this latter world. It's the world Ellis would *like* to experience – a half-remembered, half-imagined, wonderful world – and its existence complicates things. It makes the rest of life seem disappointing and frustrating, leaving young people uneasy and making it harder for them to accept the ordinary imperfections of daily life while they still imagine something better, different, extraordinary (see Chapter 12). At the height of an argument where adults are insisting that rules are rules and 'that's just the way things are', it's as if young people sometimes pause for a moment, wondering whether or not to go for broke and make that wonderful, half-remembered world their prize. Sometimes they do decide to go for it and break all the rules, refusing to accept 'the way things are': they 'lose it', thrashing about and screaming, returning briefly to an infantile state (Luxmoore 2006). 'All our stories are about what happens to our wishes,' writes Phillips (1998). 'About the world as we would like it to be, and the world as it happens to be, irrespective of our wishes and despite our hopes' (p.1). In as much as this book is about sameness and difference, it's also about young people living with this tension between the way things are and the way things might be (see Chapter 10).

Adults are caught up in this tension as well, as Chapter 14 describes. Yalom (2008) writes that 'The death anxiety of many people is fuelled… by disappointment at never having fulfilled their potential. Many people are in despair because their dreams didn't come true, and they despair even more that they did not make them come true' (p.140). When parents sense that their own opportunities to be different or to be extraordinary have now passed, it's tempting for them to live vicariously through their children, deriding anything that smacks of failure. As Phillips (1998) goes on, it's as if 'I am humiliated at that moment when I can no longer bear… the disparity between who I seem to be and who I want to be' (pp.95–6).

Monty Python's famous 'Four Yorkshiremen' sketch captures that disparity. Four smug, middle-aged businessmen sit back, puffing on cigars, enormously pleased with their success and competing with each other as to who's come from the humblest background. They tell ridiculous stories of childhood deprivation, exaggerating wildly, their stories becoming more and more ludicrous in an attempt to make their subsequent success all the more remarkable. Their professed belief in the good, old-fashioned virtue of poverty is undone by their obvious pleasure in escaping that poverty. The contradiction is funny.

There are plenty of people like the four Yorkshiremen whose success or whose celebrity we resent and despise from afar. Only a few of them do we love and we call these people 'national treasures'. They're brilliant at what they do and, like other famous people, they're feted for doing it. But there's an ordinariness about them, a sense that underneath all the fame and wealth and glamour, they cry and swear and make mistakes and go to the toilet like the rest of us. Their ordinariness is somehow transparent and we love them for it, reassured to know that, whatever their successes, they share a 'common' humanity with us, no better or worse than we are.

Living with ordinariness means holding a balance between 'I should be more than I think I am' and 'I fear I may be less than I think I am'. This book describes young people's continual attempts to hold some sort of balance. With help.

A Story about Difference

On the same day that a racist street killing preoccupied the national media, an entire year group of 280 school students sat in stunned silence, listening to an assembly about the horrors of the Holocaust. Then, later in the week, one of those students was overheard calling another a 'Paki bastard' as they stood in the queue for lunch, two were caught smearing chewing gum into the hair of a boy they thought was gay and another student was punched for having red hair.

As the counsellor in the school, I was contacted and invited to 'do something'.

I like working in schools because I think it's possible to promote cultures where this kind of behaviour is less likely to happen – behaviour which, unchecked, has been responsible for humanity's worst atrocities. Like other professionals, my work has no direct bearing on the destiny of nations but, working with those professionals, I can begin to affect one very small bit of one very small nation – a single school in a single town which (as far as I know) has never known racial segregation or the lynching of homosexuals but a town, like most, where all manner of racist and homophobic suggestions can be heard from time to time.

Whenever I hear about incidents like these (the racist insult, the chewing gum in the hair, the punching), I feel angry and useless. I worry that I should be doing more to prevent these things from happening, and I'm sure that my colleagues feel similarly because, whenever their best efforts seem to have made no difference, they cast around for someone who hasn't yet had a go – in this case, me! The email explained that these incidents had all happened in the same week and that I might like to 'do something' with this particular year group of students – the implication being that, for once, I might like to do something *practical* rather than sit on my backside all day listening to people's problems!

So I was free if I wanted to make impassioned pleas about tolerance to other assemblies. I could arrange to see the culprits and make them feel even more guilty. I could start running groups about homophobia and racism, 'And so you see, boys and girls, homophobia is bad and racism is bad also!' I could send selected students off to conferences about homophobia in schools. I could find out when the next national anti-racist week was happening and put up all the posters… At least then I'd be *doing something*.

There'd be no harm in any of these ideas but none of them would make much difference. Of course, there's always a place for practical action whenever bullying behaviour happens, and these three incidents were all examples of bullying. Someone has to punish the behaviour appropriately and make it clear what will happen if it continues. But the teachers would already have done that, quite properly. By now the bullying students would know perfectly well that their behaviour was wrong. They'd have agreed that homophobia and racism were bad and would have repeatedly assured their teachers that they were neither homophobic nor racist.

None of this practical action would have affected their underlying anxiety – the anxiety provoking their behaviour in the first place – because knowing something in our heads ('Bullying Is Wrong') doesn't necessarily mean that we behave any differently towards other people when we're afraid or jealous or suspicious of them. Our anxiety gets the better of us and we quickly project that anxiety onto our victims, saying that *he's* small or *she's* stupid or *he's* ugly or *she's* useless. There's usually a mismatch between what we know and how we behave.

'You'll be aware that we've had a spate of these incidents in the last few days. We've taken action and warned the culprits about what to expect if it happens again but would it be possible for you to do something?'

I did do something. It wasn't the most startlingly original thing to do and it was certainly no panacea. But it was something.

Taking advice, I approached those students and teachers generally considered to be the ones most respected by everyone else, whether for good or bad reasons, whether they were diligent eleven-year-olds or truculent seventeen-year-olds, whether they were cool young teachers or wise old teachers. I spoke to the baddest boy in the school; I spoke to the headteacher and I spoke to all sorts of other key people because, rightly or wrongly, they were the ones with influence.

I invited each of them to tell me something about themselves which made them different from other people. I explained that my plan was to write up whatever they said as a paragraph with their name at the bottom. They could write the paragraph themselves if they wanted. Each paragraph had to begin, 'One thing that makes me different from other people is...' I asked them to be as honest as possible within the bounds of confidentiality and decency because anyone and everyone would potentially be reading whatever they'd written in the booklet I would publish containing all these paragraphs.

No one baulked at the idea. Sometimes we sat down and wrote the paragraph together there and then; sometimes people went away to think about it and I waited for their paragraph to come back...

My thinking was that if I could get these culturally important people to acknowledge their own differences as honestly as possible, then it might help others feel less anxious about being different and less inclined to project that anxiety onto other people in the form of bullying – 'You're a Paki! You're gay! You've got red hair!' Anxieties about difference are at the heart of homophobia, racism and all sorts of other, persecutory behaviours. Because we secretly fear being different from other people and because other people remind us of parts of ourselves which feel somehow 'different', we're likely to feel less fearful if the people we most respect and admire seem unconcerned about their own particular kinds of difference.

Excitingly honest paragraphs came back, all beginning, 'One thing that makes me different from other people is…' and finishing that sentence with statements such as, 'I'm mixed race… I lost my mother at the age of nine due to cancer… I get night terrors… I'm Irish… I'm Zimbabwean… I'm adopted… I'm a practising Christian… I'm foreign… I hate being overweight… I never saw much of my biological father who died recently… I'm diabetic… I've moved school five times… I spoke fluent Bengali until I was five… my mum and dad split up when I was four…' Each contributor went on to describe the significance of this particular experience in their lives.

Someone designed a cover and, with all the paragraphs typed up, I printed the booklet without any introduction, without any school logos or other signs of institutional ownership. The paragraphs were arranged in no particular order with student and teacher authors alongside one another, distinguishable only by name – the implication being that these people were all human beings deserving of respect, regardless of their age or status within the school.

There was no formal launch or fanfare. I simply left copies of the booklet lying around in canteens, classrooms, libraries, toilets – wherever people gathered. And I watched as they were devoured – read on the spot or stashed away in bags and taken off to be read elsewhere – stolen, in effect. I overheard them being discussed, 'Have you seen this…? Oh my god, I never knew…! That's so true…! Aaah, bless him…! That's just like my dad…! God, I'd never have the guts to write anything like that…!' Because the authors were so well respected and were daring to be honest, there was no cynicism. Some people told me that they'd been moved to tears by what they'd read, and several authors told me about people they'd never met before coming up and speaking to them about the booklet.

Every few days, I went round putting out fresh supplies as the booklets continued to disappear.

Perhaps we should have found some way of evaluating the effectiveness of this booklet as a particular kind of intervention. But we didn't. It was intended to be subversive, without the usual institutional trappings and without a sense of 'And so you see, boys and girls...' It was intended to model a degree of honesty in the hope that the *experience* of reading about the lives of the people we all knew well would affect everyone more than another round of well-meaning, didactic assemblies. As an intervention, it would have been very difficult to evaluate because it was only one of many things affecting the prevailing culture in the school. I like to think that this prevailing culture is now a little more tolerant of difference, but my sense of this is highly subjective and, of course, as the counsellor, I have a vested interest in believing it to be the case.

Otherness

The students involved in the bullying incidents described in Chapter 2 were all perfectly intelligent, so why, despite all that they'd heard about the Holocaust in their assembly, couldn't they have recognised the wrongness of their behaviour? They weren't criminal or psychopathic or 'bad' in any way. They hadn't been persecuted or given reason to feel especially bitter about their lives. They were simply young people made anxious by difference.

That anxiety is primitive, taking us back to a time before words when, as babies, we begin to differentiate between ourselves and the world around us. 'Is this hand that I'm sucking part of me? Or is it my mother's breast? Is she part of me? Am I part of her? Where do I end and other people begin?' Balindt (1968) describes this environment as initially:

> undifferentiated; on the one hand, there are as yet no objects in it; on the other hand, it has hardly any structure, in particular no sharp boundaries towards the individual; environment and individual penetrate into each other, they exist together in a 'harmonious mix-up'. (p.66)

He uses the example of water in the gills of a fish… Is the water part of the fish or part of the sea?

This process of distinguishing between what Winnicott (1965) calls 'Me and Not Me' is gradual as we move from being merged with our mothers to being physically and psychologically separate. It's a nerve-wracking process – venturing out and retreating, venturing out again and retreating again, learning what's safe to touch and what bites, who to trust and who to fear. Freud (1921/2001) writes that we move 'from an absolutely self-sufficient narcissism to the perception of a changing external world and the beginnings of the discovery of objects' (p.130). The 'objects' we discover as we look around are other people. It's a process which is both exciting and frightening as we swing between differing reactions to the *otherness* of these people, curious about them one minute and terrified of them the next.

Thirteen or more years later, most young people have begun to accept that this process will always be hazardous: they'll always be partly in control and partly not in control; power will always have to be shared with other people and with the environment. They're learning to live with this. But there are times when they lose confidence, when a temporary equilibrium is disturbed and they revert to a much more primitive, baby-like position, falling back either on frightened paranoia ('I give up! I'm tiny, powerless and completely controlled by other people!') or swaggering grandiosity ('I'm the whole world! I'm in charge and I control everybody!'). Parents and professionals might recognise sons and daughters swinging loudly between 'Just tell me what to do!' and 'You can't tell me what to do!' There are sulks, tears and furious arguments as the boundaries between 'Me and Not Me' are fought over, negotiated, fought over again and re-negotiated.

It's a slow process, learning how and when to share, when to insist on independence and when to allow other people close. Young people are wrestling with an experience of the world's otherness, even when they're apparently coping perfectly well with an everyday world of parents, siblings, friends and school. They remain fascinated and appalled by extreme examples of otherness: dinosaurs, ghosts, monsters, aliens from outer space, vampires, weirdos, spiders, rats, insects, supernatural beings... Kafka's *Metamorphosis* (1916/1961) is effectively a cautionary tale for young people fascinated by otherness but afraid of becoming 'other' themselves. Waking up one morning in his bedroom, a young man finds himself inexplicably trapped in the body of a huge insect. He can no longer communicate with his parents who find their new insect-son repulsive. His physical difference and emotional separation from them is awful and yet there's nothing whatsoever that he can do about it. His parents no longer recognise him as their son. He's an insect now – forever different.

For young people holed up in their bedrooms and feeling different, feeling alien, Kafka's story might be about them. Their fascination with all things 'weird' (Luxmoore 2000) stems from a fear of being weird themselves with no one to understand, no one to share that experience. It's frightening, and all young people have moments when they sense the loneliness of the alien, the social outcast, the person who's different. 'Solitude, psychological solitude, is the mother of anxiety,' writes Wolf (1980, p.128). They dread that solitude and will do anything to avoid it, steering clear of any peers who are thought of as loners or 'losers', checking all the time that their friends are still their friends, that their own emerging likes and dislikes are understood by other people and are socially acceptable.

I remember driving twelve boys to a notorious area of the city. They'd heard about it but had never been there even though it was only eight miles away from where they lived. In their own surroundings, these were the tough boys, the boys who swaggered and swore and held sway. But here, they looked out of the minibus, intrigued and intimidated by the unfamiliar people on the pavements. Those pointing were urged by their friends not to do so in case anyone outside saw and came after our rickety minibus. I remember one boy saying, 'God, I hope we don't break down here!'

Like the bullying students with their racism and homophobia, an anxiety about otherness never entirely goes away. There's always something upon which it can be focused. If not dinosaurs, monsters or aliens from outer space, then everyday pets provide young people with opportunities to explore a relationship with otherness. 'To what extent does my dog understand me? To what extent are we merged? To what extent does she feel like I feel? To what extent is she "just a dog" and to what extent is she "part of the family"? When she dies, should we grieve for her as a lost relative or should we think of her merely as a heap of bones belonging to another species?'

There's a sense in which young people always bring to counselling some experience of otherness with which they're stuck. Occasionally they do talk about pets but, one way or another, they end up talking about the otherness of other people – the people who try to control them or the people they try to control. They're upset and perplexed by the strangeness of other people's behaviour (Luxmoore 2000). Libby complains that her step-mother is 'so weird'. Nelson says that his dad 'isn't acting like a dad'. Sneha admits that she can't understand her sister. Mack is baffled by a new teacher who's 'just so different'.

An experience of otherness extends to relationships with counsellors. In dealing with what Winnicott (1975) calls 'the task of reality acceptance', counselling offers young people 'an intermediate area of experience' where they can safely explore the ebb and flow between 'Me and Not Me'. For some, my otherness as a counsellor is interesting and they ask questions, wanting to know about my family and where I live. I tell them as much as I'm happy for them to know. When they want more, I explain that I keep some things private because that's what people do: there are degrees of privacy (Luxmoore 2000). For some, my otherness is a source of hope ('I know you'll understand!') while, for others, thinking about me as an autonomous, separate, 'other' person with a life of his own is too much to contemplate: they sit down, barely acknowledging my presence, saying nothing or shutting me out by launching into an extended monologue. For them, my otherness is evidently a source of despair ('There's no way you'll understand!').

We keep going and our conversations develop, but usually I'm a reminder of far more important people in their lives. Ultimately, the hope and the despair are focused on the otherness of their parents because it's with these people that any young person's struggle with otherness begins: 'What do I have in common with these people? Are they really my parents? Am I as different from them as I feel? In what ways am I like them? In what ways do I *want* to be like them?' Our parents are fascinating and appalling, desirable and dangerous. Young people talking about their 'parents' refer both to an original, internalised experience of safety and danger, nurture and neglect, merger and separation which goes right back to the beginning of their lives as well as to those external, day-to-day humans with whom they currently live and fight.

Jodi, for example, is fighting with her parents over bedtimes, friends and computer use. The boundaries her parents (quite properly) erect to keep their daughter safe are experienced by Jodi as a hostile kind of otherness, thwarting and confining her: 'They never let me do anything! It's always what *they* want to do! I mean, for god's sake, I'm fifteen!'

We talk a lot about her mother who is evidently the person most insistent on curfews and bedtimes. Jodi rages. Her father isn't so bad, she says, 'At least he understands that I've got to have a bit of freedom! I overheard him one time telling Mum that she was being hard on me...'

Our conversation can do absolutely nothing to change her parents or their rules. All I can do is to help Jodi think more flexibly about the situation and, so far, we've established that 'my parents' are actually two people with slightly different approaches. Their otherness is no longer straightforward and so there's already a sense that, within the parental couple, there's the possibility of understanding (from her father) as well as punishment (from her mother).

We keep talking. Jodi mentions that her mother has recently been contacted after many years by her daughter from a relationship which finished long before Jodi's mother met Jodi's father.

I ask how old her mother was when she gave birth to this long-lost daughter.

'Fifteen,' Jodi says, then stares at me. 'Oh my god! And I'm fifteen and my mum's trying to stop me seeing boys!'

A child might experience a mother as kind or cruel, good or bad – one thing or the other. Jodi is starting to understand her mother's otherness as more complex than that – informed by motivations and needs which aren't solely to do with Jodi. It seems that her mother's insistence on Jodi being back home by a certain time is no longer simply a matter of spite or of some arbitrary determination to thwart Jodi at all costs. In fact, with this realisation about her mother's past, Jodi can begin to understand and even sympathise with one aspect of her mother's 'otherness' and can start wondering whether her mother's behaviour towards her – while annoying – is quite as deliberately persecutory as it always feels.

Mason alternates between experiencing his parents as *like* him when they stick up for him against his brothers and *unlike* him when they nag at him or refuse to let him have his own way. He experiences their 'otherness' as changeable, feeling sometimes that his mother is like him and his father unlike him and, at other times, feeling as if it's the other way round. Sometimes their otherness feels supportive and interested (he 'likes' them) and at other times it feels hostile and persecutory (he 'dislikes' them). 'They're weird,' he says. 'I don't see why they have to be so annoying when they can be nice if they want to be!'

'Maybe that's how people are, Mason.'

He frowns. 'Doesn't make sense. Why can't they just be nice all the time?'

Pointing out that nobody is 'nice' all the time and that we have to get used to people as they are might well be true but would be a worthless observation. In our meetings, Mason has an opportunity to reflect on his experience of other people – the ups and downs, satisfactions and dissatisfactions – as he learns to live with their alikeness and unalikeness, their essential *otherness*.

This might seem like a far cry from a baby establishing Me and Not Me but I think Mason and Jodi and so many other young people are always re-visiting and re-interpreting that original experience. The sense of otherness that a baby experiences in relation to its parents is bound – years later – to inform a young person's experience of flawed parents trying their best to get it right for their teenage son or daughter. Jodi's and Mason's parents will be like them in some ways and unlike them in others. Understanding and living with this inescapable fact will be a crucial part of any young person's development.

Trying to Be Interesting

The otherness of parents is one thing but, like anyone waking up in an insect's body and feeling alien, young people's *own* otherness is equally perplexing: 'Is it me or is it my parents? Are they the weird ones or am I?' A lot of young people's energy goes into proving that it's *other* people who are the weird ones, but they're intrigued and perturbed by the possibility of their own otherness nonetheless. Some display a particular difference or otherness for all the world to see – dressing up flamboyantly, moulding their hair into the most unusual styles or making themselves look as offensive or unconventional as possible, deliberately identifying themselves with whatever will attract the greatest public outrage. Others do the opposite, hiding behind a mask of shyness, shunning the limelight, trying to be invisible and blending into the background at every opportunity.

Young people are always aware that there's a part of themselves capable of being outrageously, publicly different, and another part capable of hiding, desperate not to stand out from the crowd. They're well aware of peers who most obviously represent such extreme behaviours and, whether they're flamboyantly different ('Who the hell does he think he is?') or entirely anonymous ('She's such a nonentity!'), both behaviours are scorned.

In his book about the killings in 1999 at Columbine High School, Cullen (2009) describes one of the two teenage murderers as a psychopath and the other, Dylan Klebold, as a mixed-up kid. Drawing on Dylan's journal, Cullen writes:

> Dylan was unique, that much he was sure of. He had been watching the kids at school. Some were good, some bad, but all so utterly different from him. Dylan exceeded even Eric in his belief in his own singularity. But Eric equated 'unique' with 'superior' – Dylan saw it mostly as bad. Unique meant lonely. What good were special talents when there was no one to share them with?
>
> His moods came and went quickly. Dylan turned compassionate, then fatalistic. "I don't fit in here," he complained. But the road to the afterlife was just monstrous: "go to school, be scared & nervous, hoping that people can accept me." (p.175)

It's hard for young people to know how to understand and interpret their own 'singularity' or otherness. Schools give mixed messages. A school uniform, for example, suggests that sameness is desirable. Teachers put hours into enforcing 'the uniform', reprimanding and punishing any students who depart from the norm because everyone must look the same. But there's an opposite injunction. I remember sitting at the back of an assembly, watching a short film in which wide-eyed children around the world in houses, shacks and tents were watching the Olympics on television and dreaming of winning a gold medal. By cleverly superimposing faces onto the children as they grew older and eventually won medals themselves, the film suggested that 'You, too, have it in you to be the champion!' – an encouragement to stand out from the crowd, to be different, unique.

I'm not criticising schools with uniforms or motivational films about the Olympics because I think this conflict between sameness and difference is inevitable for all young people regardless of whether they go to schools with uniforms or sit in assemblies watching films about the Olympics. As I described in the last chapter, it's a conflict which goes back to a baby's earliest experiences of the world's otherness. Somehow a baby has to attract its mother's attention in order to be looked after and survive. It has to be recognised by her and *interest* her. Initially, a baby might do this through perpetual, anxious screaming – the only way it knows. But over time that anxiety lessens as its mother continues to respond and as the baby develops a sense of being intrinsically interesting without having to scream all the time. Now it can writhe and smile and frown and gurgle under its mother's gaze, enjoying her attention, responding to her prompts and, in turn, prompting her to respond to its own developing repertoire of gestures. 'Look how interesting I am! And you're interesting, too!'

I remember one young person complaining to me, 'I don't want to be part of the crowd! I want to be noticed!' This had been a recurring theme in our conversations. She went on, 'I was walking home through the cemetery last week and I was reading all the stuff on the tombstones and I walked back the next day and realised that I couldn't remember anything I'd read the day before! It was like I'd forgotten about all those people…' Her life story had been about trying to be noticed. 'I don't want to be forgotten!'

The extent to which young people experience themselves as intrinsically interesting (or noticeable or unforgettable) will be the extent to which they can then find it in themselves to be interested in the otherness of other people: 'Because I know I'm interesting, I can therefore afford to be interested in you!' For someone else's otherness to be unthreatening, a young person needs to know that his or her own otherness is enjoyable not repulsive, understandable not weird. Young people need to know that they're interesting.

It's a word they use all the time: 'I'm not interested… You're not interested in me… It wasn't interesting… I can't get interested…' and, by extension, 'This is boring… I'm so bored… You're boring me…' Being boring (the thing young people fear) means being unrecognised and losing someone's interest. Those young people trying so hard to be outrageous might really just be young people trying hard to be interesting while shy, withdrawn young people might be young people who have given up on the possibility of ever being interesting to anybody.

When we sense that other people are interested in us, we come alive. But awkward, unconfident Kwami reports that his friends don't seem interested in anything he has to say. Instead, they tease him. 'That's the only reason they let me go round with them,' he says, 'so that they've got someone to make jokes about.'

He's probably right. In mocking Kwami, his friends mock and distance themselves from all the social and sexual awkwardness he represents. He's useful to the group as the object of their projections – the scapegoat – but their behaviour leaves him unhappy and disheartened.

I mention girls.

'They wouldn't be interested in me,' he says quickly.

His shoulders are hunched. He avoids my eye and often avoids my questions, preferring to continue a monologue of his own, seemingly unaware that he's losing my interest. I learn to avoid asking about films or computer games because, given half a chance, he'll start telling me the whole plot in mechanical detail without distinguishing between any of the characters and without anyone's feelings being involved. He doesn't discriminate between what's important and what's unimportant. It's as if Kwami has no idea how to make himself interesting to me. Describing his experiences as a hospital patient, the famously self-effacing Alan Bennett (2005) writes:

> Nothing excuses us from the obligation to divert our fellow creatures. We must not be boring. And since for the specialist most illnesses soon cease to intrigue, if you have to suffer choose a condition that is rare. Should you want to catch the doctor's eye, the trick is not to see no light at the end of the tunnel; anybody can do that. Rather mistake your wife for a hat and the doctor will never go away from your bedside. (p.34)

Presumably Kwami imagines that the details of an action film will interest me because he could never be interesting to me in his own right. So until he experiences himself (his otherness) as interesting, he'll continue to merge into this group of so-called friends, afraid to disagree with them, afraid to stand up for himself, afraid to be different or alone. It'll be difficult for him to accept my interested attention because he'll also be well aware of the scorn attracted by young people trying to be different or insisting on their own otherness. 'Tall Poppy Syndrome' describes the scorn we heap on those people who do extremely well or who seem to think that they're better than the rest of us. 'He's only seeking attention!' we complain. 'She just wants attention! They're always trying to get attention!'

We talk about young people 'seeking attention' as if it was the worst thing in the world – something shameful and unimaginable. But whoever we are, our need for attention never changes because, without the attention and recognition of other people, it's as if we don't exist. As babies, we only know we exist and matter because other people recognise us, understand what we're saying and respond to us (Luxmoore 2008). Usually, we've absorbed enough of other people's attention in the early years of our lives to feel that we exist and matter without needing constant reassurance. But there are young people like Kwami who haven't absorbed enough of this.

We talk about his life at home. His two elder brothers are good at everything, he says. His mum and dad are always taking them to weekend study camps, football training, orchestra rehearsals, parties.

'I'm just average.'

I ask what it's like to be average.

'Don't know, really. Never really thought about it.'

He starts telling me about a programme on television last night. I gear myself up for another boringly detailed account of the plot, but this time a metaphor comes to my rescue. Apparently, the man in the story was trying to escape from prison, having been unjustly sentenced for a crime he didn't commit.

'Sounds like you,' I say, knowing full well that Kwami won't understand.

He stops in his tracks. 'What do you mean?'

'I mean a man imprisoned because people don't understand, because they don't believe him, because no one takes any notice of what he says…'

He looks embarrassed. 'What? And you think I'm like that?'

'Maybe a bit…? Like, people not taking any notice? Like you feeling like giving up sometimes? Starting to think they must be right?'

He thinks about this. 'But I'm not in prison!'

'Aren't you?'

'Oh, I see what you mean! Yeah, I suppose I am in a way. You mean with my friends?'

Counselling involves one person seeking attention and another person paying attention – *really* paying attention, *really* trying to understand and *really* trying to stay attuned (Caldwell 2007). It involves paying attention to what's *not* being said as much as to what is – paying attention to how angry the person's feeling, how unfair things seem to be, how lonely and sad the person gets, how responsible he's become, how childlike and stupid he sometimes feels, how difficult it is to deal with other people…

Kwami doesn't tell me any of these things because he doesn't think I'll be interested. Instead, he asks for advice about what he should do to get his friends to back off. 'They're always on my case! Always taking the piss!'

We talk about how he feels when he's with them – his anger, helplessness, humiliation. I offer no solutions or strategies but clearly I'm interested.

'My mum says I should ignore them.'

'And you say?'

'I say it's not that easy! You can't just ignore them when they're going on at you all the time!' He slips into talking about himself in the second person.

'What's your mum like?'

'She's okay…' He looks down, indignation subsiding, energy draining away. It's as if he becomes boring again at the mention of his mother. 'What do you want me to say?'

'Whatever you like…'

'Don't know, really. She's my mum.'

We go on to talk about her and I encourage him to tell me all the things he *feels* like saying to her, offering him an experience of telling his feelings and practising for assertive conversations he may or may not have with her in the future. This is all good therapeutic stuff, expanding the kind of relationship Kwami can have with his mother (the mother in his mind if not his actual mother) and potentially giving him back some of the confidence she may have inadvertently taken away from him. What I can't help him to change is his original experience of himself as an interesting or boring baby. At the time, his parents may well have been preoccupied with their elder sons and may have taken the new baby for granted. But that's speculation. All I can do is to give Kwami an experience of himself as interesting *now* – interesting whenever I say hello in the school canteen and he mumbles back, surprised that anyone should have noticed him; interesting every time he shuffles into my counselling room and, monosyllabic at first, begins to talk. These experiences can be set against an abiding sense of being boring, helping to amend that old belief.

Ordinariness and Extraordinariness

Worrying about young people obliged to watch films which imply that they're all capable of becoming Olympic champions isn't the same as condoning under-achievement. Ambitions are important, and no one should be denied opportunities because of their gender, race, sexuality, disability or socio-economic circumstances – I believe that passionately. In fact, I think we have a moral duty to help young people live their lives as fully as possible. But at the same time, there's nothing wrong with being ordinary, and to encourage young people (all desperate to be interesting) in the belief that they're extraordinary or *should be* extraordinary is unfair.

Schools and other organisations develop this expectation of young people because, as institutions, they develop a collective anxiety about whether they themselves are ordinary or extraordinary. There's a rhetoric, driven by capitalism and by post-Enlightenment notions of predictability and control, whereby relentless improvement is not only possible but is the only thing that counts. If you've done well, then set higher targets. If you achieve those, then set targets which are higher still. For schools and for non-statutory organisations competing for funding, there are political pressures to appear extraordinarily good and to hide from the public gaze anything 'merely' ordinary. 'Excellence' has become an obligatory word in organisational rhetoric. Every year, schools are obliged to claim that their latest exam results are, in some particularly gratifying way, excellent – indeed, exceptional.

But what happens when you've worked as hard as possible and the exam results *aren't* as good as the year before? Does that make the people involved failures? Does it mean that they were lazy or complacent? Does it mean (in football parlance) that they didn't 'want it' enough? Does it mean that professionals should start blaming each other and seeking out imaginary backsliders? Does it mean focusing even more narrowly on exams at the expense of everything else? In cases where a school's exam results have been genuinely outstanding, I think that school enters a period of increased anxiety, wondering how on earth it can improve on these results if relentless improvement has become the political order of the day. Extraordinariness creates anxiety rather than happiness.

In Peter Shaffer's (1980) play *Amadeus*, the talented and successful court-composer Salieri is confronted by an obnoxious young man called Mozart who seems to have a God-given gift. Salieri realises that his own music pales in comparison with Mozart's and yet there's nothing whatsoever that he can do about it. Try as he does to accept the unfairness of this young man's extraordinary musical ability in comparison with his own ordinary talent, he can't. He feels empty, vengeful, knowing that the very existence of Mozart's music condemns him and his music to be 'forever mediocre'. Having worked hard all his life, he wonders what he's done to deserve this ignominy, this apparent punishment from God. If only Mozart was dead!

The play is about coming to terms with ordinariness. Like Salieri, young people wrestle with the Mozarts in their heads. 'If I'm not and can't be extraordinary, then what's the point of my life? Am I okay as I am or should I be better than I am?' There are endless talent shows on television looking for performers with the mysterious 'X factor'. Thousands of young people queue to audition, all reciting the same mantra, 'This means everything to me… It's the most important thing in my life… If I can't do this, then I've got nothing – I don't know what I'll do with my life!'

and thousands are rejected every week for being ordinary. Only a few make it through to the last rounds of the competition where every week the superlatives increase, the lights flash ever more brightly and the audience is encouraged to believe that this week's winners are even more extraordinary than last week's.

In 2009, a middle-aged woman called Susan Boyle appeared on one of these shows in the UK. Stocky and plump, she shuffled onstage in an ill-fitting dress, embarrassingly confident and obviously intending to sing.

The audience smirked and sniggered.

There was a hush. Slowly, the music began. Slowly, she started to sing and to everyone's amazement her voice was wonderful – clear and strong and operatic. In fact, her voice was quite beautiful. Quickly the audience was clapping, cheering, weeping, realising its dreadful assumption, its dreadful mistake and humbled that someone who looked so ordinary could sing so beautifully.

This moment was eventually watched by millions on the internet. School assemblies went into overdrive, especially when it was revealed that Susan Boyle had 'learning difficulties'. As with films about the Olympics, it seemed that anything was possible. Anyone could be Susan Boyle.

Commenting in *The Guardian*, Libby Brooks described 'The Susan Boyle myth... the fantasy of exceptionalism' whereby children and young people are supposed to rescue themselves from disadvantage by discovering some previously untapped talent. She wrote:

> The children that this country has most difficulty accepting are those... described as the 'unexceptional disadvantaged', the ones who can't dance or act or paint their way out of the cycle of deprivation... it is not everyone's moral duty to have a gift. (Brooks 2009)

Talent shows are effectively a national exploration of whether we're ordinary or extraordinary. Do we have the 'X factor' ourselves and, if we don't, are we worth anything? Karaoke competitions abound in clubs and holiday resorts because we're still not sure how seriously to take ourselves as singers. We may get drunk before staggering on stage and we may pretend to be ridiculous but secretly we're uncertain. Maybe, just maybe…? And okay, maybe we don't have beautiful voices but maybe we have other hidden talents?

For young people, the problem of ordinariness affects everything. I remember a boy once telling me that he no longer felt excited when he saw his girlfriend. He no longer felt butterflies in his stomach and was worried that this might mean he was no longer in love with her because what he felt no longer seemed so extraordinary. We talked about the possibility that real love might be ordinary and slow and reliable and clumsy and cumulative; that the very ordinariness of his love might be what made it valuable.

Against this background of wondering whether they're ordinary or extraordinary, young people are endlessly trying to gauge whether they're achieving the 'personal potential' that adults speak about all the time (Luxmoore 2008). As a result, they're constantly comparing themselves with each other and wondering, 'Would it matter if I went to this university rather than that one? And if I don't go to any university, does that make me a failure? Is it okay to leave school and get a job in the bakery? Or the garage? Or working with old people? Would it be more fun to be friends with this person rather than that person? Should I be going to more parties, having more exotic holidays? And if I don't become an Olympic champion, is that because I'm lazy?'

There's a popular saying that if you work hard enough and want something badly enough, you'll get it. The third president of the United States, Thomas Jefferson, is often quoted, 'Nothing on earth can stop the man with the right mental attitude from reaching his goal; nothing on earth can help the man with the wrong mental attitude.' It sounds so simple – just change your mental attitude! Believe you can do it! Young people are told this sort of stuff all the time and it's simply untrue. Wanting it *isn't* enough.

We denigrate ordinariness and deify extraordinariness. Brilliant poets are supposedly blessed by 'the muse'; amazing talents are described as 'God-given'. Gladwell (2008) offers an alternative view. He describes the way in which the most astonishingly successful people – including Mozart – have talent for sure but manage to achieve what they do through hard work, accidents of birth, parental support and being in the right place at the right time; *not* through some innate, extraordinary 'genius':

> Superstar lawyers and math wizzes and software entrepreneurs appear at first blush to lie outside ordinary experience. But they don't. They are the products of history and community, of opportunity and legacy. Their success is not exceptional or mysterious. It is grounded in a web of advantages and inheritances, some deserved, some not, some earned, some just plain lucky – but all of them critical in making them who they are. (p.285)

It's not that some of us have got it and others haven't, therefore. Our talents are relative: we're more or less talented at all sorts of different things and we can improve.

This matters because if we're all supposed to be extraordinary, achieving extraordinary things and living extraordinary lives, then we're doomed to failure. What happens when we've worked as hard as possible and wanted it as much as possible and *still* things haven't gone according to the impossible plan? What then? Despair? Depression? Does it mean that our lives have been pointless? Wasted? When young people's expectations are unrealistic and the Olympic title eludes them, the disappointment can be shattering. Judging oneself against a criterion of relentless improvement is dangerous. If a school or young person's sense of worth is bound up with relentless improvement, then the flipside is abject failure and despair. Research by Wood, Perunovic and Lee (2009) suggests that trying to convince people with 'low self-esteem' to think positively about themselves ('I *am* clever! I *am* loveable! I *can* do this…') only reinforces their negative view of themselves. I'm not surprised. My guess would be that the discrepancy between a young person's habitual lack of confidence and other people's exhortations to do better! better! better! becomes so great that most young people can't make any connection between how they feel and how they're supposed to feel. Ehrenreich (2009) describes the simplistic but widespread assumption that 'positive thinking' will somehow replace misfortune and misery with success and popularity. 'There is a vast difference,' she points out, 'between positive thinking and existential courage' (p.6).

For parents and professionals, the task is less about convincing young people of their extraordinary potential and more about helping them to enjoy and value being ordinary where 'being ordinary' means balancing the things they can do well with the things they can't do so well. That *doesn't* mean being mediocre. As I've said, the thought of 'mere' ordinariness haunts young people more than they'll admit. They'll deride other people's efforts to better themselves and insist that they're absolutely satisfied with their own lives. But they're intrigued by successful people and they're envious. They wonder if it's still too late to be discovered by some mysterious talent scout who might just be around the corner, looking for the extraordinary person with the X factor.

Cara told me that she was a good singer and I said I was pleased. She explained that there'd been a singing contest at the holiday resort and she'd won the competition for her age group. She even had the certificate and photograph to prove it.

Again, I said I was pleased and encouraged her to audition for the school musical.

She said she'd think about it.

When I asked again, a week later, she said that she was still thinking about it. When I asked *again* after the deadline for auditions had passed, she told me that she'd turned up for her audition but the teacher was busy and hadn't had time to hear her sing. And so, just because of that, Cara said, she was now going to miss out on 'getting a really big part' in the show. It was so unfair.

I think she never went to the audition. Or if she did, she somehow managed to sabotage things by being rude or half-hearted so that the teacher didn't realise that she was actually there to audition. This way, Cara could blame the world for thwarting her ambitions rather than face up to her own ambivalence about putting herself forward. Of course, being in the school musical would have been wonderful for her, but she needed to take the first step herself and was still unready, caught in two minds, 'Am I ordinary or extraordinary, *really*? And if I'm ordinary, is there any point in auditioning?'

I worried whether her curiosity about being extraordinary would now get displaced into other projects – sex, pregnancy, drugs, exclusion from school. When conventional dreams like getting good exam results, winning sports competitions or acting in the school musical no longer seem possible, young people don't stop wondering whether or not they're secretly extraordinary. Even as young adults, they're still anxiously changing friends, jobs, houses, cars in search of something better. After the excitement of The Big Day, marriages break up because one partner still believes that there might just be someone out there somewhere *even better* – someone more sexy, more exciting, more sympathetic…

I saw Cara on the bus several years later, long after she'd been excluded from school. Unrecognised, I sat a few seats behind her and her unsmiling boyfriend, watching as she talked anxiously to him in between answering endless phone calls. Her attention switched backwards and forwards between her boyfriend and her phone as if something momentous was just about to happen. I found myself wondering whether that was the story of her life, whether something momentous, something extraordinary was always just about to happen to Cara.

It's easy for young people to worry that something's wrong when life no longer seems new or exciting or surprising or momentous ('Nothing ever happens round here!'). There are young people who live in a perpetual state of arousal, moving from one melodrama to the next, unable to be still. For them, bearing the ordinariness of life ('This is so boring!') is made more difficult when popular culture offers only the biggest, the fastest, the sexiest, the richest, the most powerful. Life becomes either wonderful or terrible, a triumph or a disaster, as if no middle ground exists.

There are some young people who bring to counselling an extraordinary story every week. 'I might be pregnant… They think I've got diabetes… My dad might never be able to work again… We could be losing our home… My cousin's just died… It's the anniversary of my gran's heart attack…' I hear teachers complaining that with some students 'There's always *something* the matter! There always has to be *something* going on!' Bollas (1987) describes a patient using excitement to medicate herself against an underlying depression (p.54). I think this is what young people like Cara do to be interesting, to get attention, to feel better because to be still for a moment is to risk 'being boring', being a nobody.

I meet with young people who habitually use exaggeration as a defence against the awfulness of that feeling. Like a baby needing to keep its mother's interest and like Kwami in the last chapter needing to keep my interest with the plots of action films, they imagine that the only way to keep my interest is by recounting extraordinary tales in the hope that I'll never get bored and never suggest that we stop meeting.

There are other young people who tell lies. Their intention seems to be the same – to keep my interest and to keep ordinariness at bay. But the effect is always the opposite – I feel bored and irritated and wonder whether boredom and irritation are precisely the feelings that the young person can't bear, whether the defensive process of projective identification (Klein 1946) gives these feelings to me to feel on behalf of the young person I'm with.

Delicia, for example, tells me with no discernible emotion that last night she dreamed bats were attacking her and ever since waking up this morning she's been afraid that she's about to die.

We start to explore her dream. What were the bats like? Was anyone else around? Where was she? What happened next? But she's off again... She started going out with Peter Buckland (the school hunk) at the weekend but chucked him yesterday because she can't stop thinking about a boy she met on holiday and it wouldn't be fair to keep seeing Peter if she wasn't really sure.

We start to explore her feelings about Peter. What does she like about him? Who was this boy on holiday? What was he like? But again she's off... Her dad's been hitting her mum who's an alcoholic and she's terrified for her little sister who's anorexic but nobody knows about the anorexia except for Delicia...

And so on. I'm bored and irritated, unable to engage with her because I don't believe most of what she's telling me. If she were telling me about abusive situations – sexual, physical or otherwise – I wouldn't stop to wonder whether she was exaggerating or lying but would simply support her in telling her story to another professional better able to investigate. However, she doesn't tell me those stories. Hers are more bizarre. I try to think of them as metaphors but, when I test the water, she won't concede that anything is other than it seems. I wonder whether her lies represent anxieties. Why *this* lie, I ask myself. What purpose does it serve? What does it protect Delicia from?

I think her lies protect her from ordinariness. There's a mismatch between the exotic stories she tells and the flat, unemotional way in which she tells them. If she *felt* them, she'd describe them with feeling and we'd engage with each other; whereas, told in this unemotional way, the effect is that she doesn't engage with me at all, keeping an emotional distance as if protecting herself from me. I think she protects herself from my loss of interest, and yet that's precisely the effect her stories have on me: I do lose interest; her attempts to sound extraordinary are boring.

Perhaps her anxiety goes back to some original experience of not feeling interesting enough as a baby or as an elder sister whose parents may have switched their attention to their new-born younger daughter. Whether or not that's true, her need is to be understood in all her ordinariness and so, whenever there's an opportunity, I ask about the most mundane things: what she had for breakfast, what happened in the lesson before lunch, what she's writing about for her English coursework, who cut her hair, what she was watching on television last night...

She's initially scornful, as if this isn't proper counselling, though she doesn't complain because she doesn't want to lose my attention. She's clearly amazed that I'm interested in these things and, as the weeks go by, relaxes into a different kind of conversation. She seems happier. It's as if I've said to her, 'No, Delicia, I don't want to know about all these extraordinary things – I want to know about *you!*' Weeks ago, saying this to her would have sounded like criticism and, feeling humiliated, she'd have felt unable to continue coming to see me, having failed at counselling. I think I was right to go gently in the beginning but, when young people seem to be fleeing from ordinariness into flights of mendacity, the issue of when and how to intervene remains difficult.

When I met Ash for the first time, he was twelve years old, fat and clumsy and set on becoming Manchester United's goalkeeper.

'Football's my life,' he told me.

We talked about his step-father, the cause of the anxieties which were getting him into so much trouble at school. But because I was interested in it myself, we usually talked about football at some point in our conversations. He would tell me about the friends he played with, about his new boots and replica shirts and state-of-the-art goalkeeping gloves. He said he wasn't in the school team but the teacher in charge had told him that he'd have a chance of getting into the team if he kept practising.

Ash seemed completely reassured. 'It's good he said that, because I want to be a professional footballer!'

I didn't have the heart to suggest otherwise. 'What would you do if you didn't make it at Man United?'

'Don't know,' he said. 'It's all I want to do!'

We kept meeting. His behaviour in school improved and we agreed to stop.

During the next two years, he said hello whenever he passed me, usually with a football under his arm going to and from the playing field.

We started meeting again after he got into trouble for swearing at a teacher. By now he was fourteen. He remembered our old football conversations and immediately teased me about my team getting relegated.

I asked how his football was going.

'Good!'

'Still goalkeeping?'

'More outfield now,' he said. 'Full back, usually. I reckon I've got more chance of making it professionally if I play in defence because you've got to be tall to be a goalie these days.'

My heart sank. I thought he'd have grown out of this. He hadn't lost any weight and I knew that he still wasn't in the school team. So would it be kind or cruel to challenge this professional football fantasy? Did the other boys already mock him for daring to think that he might be good enough? Who was I to take away his dreams and yet, if I didn't tell him the truth, who would? 'Adulthood,' writes Phillips (1993), 'is when it begins to occur to you that you may not be leading a charmed life' (p.82). At what point in the future would everything come crashing down? And what would be the effect on Ash when that eventually happened?

He wasn't alone. Lots of other young people have unrealistic ambitions. With no academic qualifications, they want to be vets. Having once been in a play, they want to be actors. They want to be musicians having learned a few chords on the guitar.

And it's easy for other people to sneer. I decided to find out more about what becoming a professional footballer really meant for Ash.

He said he'd been round at his dad's house at the weekend, watching Man United on television. His dad supported them as well. 'Since he was a kid! It was my dad's dad who got him into it!'

'Your grandfather?'

'Yeah!'

'Does your dad still play?'

'Used to, before he injured his knee.'

'Was he any good?'

'Says he was! But loads of people say they're good at football!'

'They do,' I said, taken aback. 'They think they're better than they are.'

'That's the reason I want to be a pro,' Ash said, 'because if you're good at something you should give it a go.'

I was mystified. 'How good are you?'

'I'm okay.'

'You're not in the school team yet?'

'No, but I should be because I'm the one who always turns up to practices which is more than some people do who *are* in the team!'

I know enough about professional football to know that if you're overweight and still not in the school football team by the time you're fourteen, your chances of becoming a professional footballer are non-existent.

'What does your dad say about you becoming a pro?'

'Haven't told him yet. I want it to be a surprise.'

I wondered if this might be about more than football.

'When I'm sixteen, I'm going to pay for us to go to Manchester on my dad's birthday and we're going to go for a tour of the ground. But when we get there, all the people will be waiting with the signing-on forms and that's when my dad will get the best surprise of his life!'

I had no idea what to say. Should I squash this fantasy now?

'I know my dad'll be proud because it's what he's always dreamed about.'

'And your mum?' I couldn't think of anything else to ask.

'It's nothing to do with my mum. She'll probably be off somewhere with my step-dad and he's not interested in football at all.'

At last I was beginning to understand something of the meaning of football for Ash and, of course, it had nothing to do with football! We went back to talking about his parents, their separation when he was eight, the arrival of his step-dad, all that Ash felt at the time and had been feeling since. In a sense, I think his ambition was to be a professional *son*, loyal to his father, keeping the flame alive, fulfilling his father's dream.

'Your dad must be very proud of you…?'

'D'you think so? Why?'

'Because you're loyal to him, because you love him, because you've put up with a lot of crap from people who don't understand…'

'They certainly don't!' Ash said. 'They take the piss out of me when I play football because I'm fat.'

'But you're doing it for your dad…'

'For me as well! Even if I didn't make it in football, I'd do something good. I'd never waste my life. I could do decorating with my uncle. Or I could do building. It wouldn't matter.'

'What does your dad do?'

'Works for the electricity company. Goes all over the place, into people's houses, factories… wherever he's needed. People are always going to need electricity, aren't they!'

Professional football clearly wasn't the do-or-die ambition I thought it was but more like the dream of a relationship between a father and son – loyal, supportive, proud. My anxiety about protecting Ash from some awful realisation suddenly seemed less urgent. He'd be perfectly content working as a decorator, as a builder or for an electricity company because of this happy identification with his father.

Other young people would be less content. As Chapter 11 describes, they continually chase the dream as if searching for something lost. For them, only an Olympic medal will suffice. 'Is there any point in my life if I'm ordinary?' For them it isn't the taking part: it's the winning and, for almost all of them, that means the failing.

Not for Ash.

Special

There's a sense in which young people go to see a counsellor or psychotherapist to find out whether they're ordinary or extraordinary and what to do about it. Lomas (1973) writes:

> Those who seek out help from a psychotherapist have, in some way and in some degree, lost their capacity for ordinary living. They have come to regard themselves as special, an experience that is painful either because they feel too odd or wicked or stupid to be understood by an ordinary person, or because they feel that those around them are quite unable to appreciate their real nature: they are in a special position in that they cannot share their experience in a way that seems possible for most people. (p.16)

With his hair cut to a frightening stubble, Marlon looks at me as if to say, 'Be careful! Just because my friends come to see you for this counselling thing doesn't mean you'll get anywhere with me!' Yet it was Marlon who asked for the appointment.

He talks about getting into trouble at school and with the police, about smoking despite his asthma, about hating school and wanting to leave as soon as possible to start earning money.

I ask about his elder brother – academically talented and popular with teachers – who's just gone off to university. 'Do the two of you get compared with each other?'

'Not really… He does his thing and I do mine.'

I suggest that having asthma must be annoying.

'No, I'm used to it. Doesn't bother me.'

Good old Marlon, I think to myself – relieved to be misunderstood yet again! We keep talking. Eventually I comment that it can be difficult when people take us at face value, thinking that our tough exteriors mean that we must be tough inside when really we might be shy and loving.

Again, he blocks me with a denial and a look which tells me just how stupid I'm being.

I'm sure there's truth in all three of my suggestions. Two very different brothers are bound to be compared with each other; anyone with asthma will have feelings about it and all of us have an exterior self which protects our inner self. But just as there are young people who avoid counselling for fear of not being understood – again – so there are young people for whom the prospect of actually *being* understood by another person is frightening. For them, it might be lovely to get some attention and feel properly understood (Marlon makes an appointment) but, at the same, time it's frightening because it's unfamiliar and means that they might not be as extraordinary as they imagined (Marlon blocks my attempts at understanding). For these young people, being misunderstood is a relief (Bollas 1987) because to be understood by another person would mean being ordinary – ordinary enough to be understood.

In the same way, while most young people are desperate to be interesting, Chelsey's *fear* is of being interesting. She welcomes my suggestion that, although she behaves angrily ('Apparently I've got anger management!') and as if she doesn't care about anything, secretly she's kind and loyal and loving. When she's with me, when we're talking and she senses my interest, she can admit that all these things are true and seems delighted that someone has recognised them at last. But then she goes away and loses confidence and I have to work hard to get her back into the room. She professes to forget our appointments, but I think she gets scared. By all accounts, her real-life father takes no interest in her and so the prospect of a (male) counsellor actually finding her interesting fills her with very mixed feelings, I suspect.

With Chelsey and with Marlon, I resolve to persist, persist, persist.

Coming to terms with our essential ordinariness without becoming dismayed or depressed is one of the tasks of adolescence. 'As every child soon notices, however important he is – however beautiful or loved or clever – he is also nothing special,' writes Phillips (1998, p.99). There are countless fairy tales in which young people labour in poverty all day long, unaware that – secretly – they're princes or princesses whose lives were changed all those years ago by some act of wickedness or misfortune. At the end of the story, the true nature of the young person is revealed and they resume their rightful position, loved and adored by all. The ugly duckling is the story of a duckling teased and ostracised by other ducks until, one day, the duckling is revealed as an exotic, beautiful swan and the ducks are forced to re-think their assumptions.

In a sense, all young people who come to see me for counselling are ducklings preoccupied with their apparent ugliness and asking, 'Am I normal? How do I compare with other people? Am I secretly special?' Most tell a version of the Cinderella story in which their everyday efforts go unrecognised by a ghastly family; in which their parents do nothing whatsoever to lessen their plight and in which they're forever waiting for their prince or princess to come. Like the protagonists in fairy tales, young people are never quite sure whether they're extraordinary people hiding inside ordinary bodies, enduring ordinary lives and waiting to be discovered, or whether their ordinariness is a given, an unchanging fact of life. They suspect the latter to be the case – that they'll always be Cinderella the pauper, never the princess – yet can't quite give up on the dream of being somehow – secretly – extraordinary.

The idea of a fairy godmother powerfully affects them. Counsellors – like parents, teachers and other professionals – are expected to act as fairy godmothers, helping to transform a young person's ordinariness into something exotic and special. When we can't do that, we're apparently useless. I sometimes wonder whether gambling is just another conversation about ordinariness that young people keep having with themselves. Because they know that *someone* has to win the jackpot eventually, they're intrigued by the possibility that maybe, maybe this time… Similarly, they run up debts and take all sorts of risks, forever toying with the idea that a fairy godmother will somehow emerge at the last minute to save them from the ordinariness of personal responsibility.

Counsellors refer to these fairy godmother beliefs as 'magical thinking'. Freud (1912) associates magical thinking with what he calls 'primary narcissism' (1914) – a baby's original belief that he or she is everything and controls everything. We grow up and usually grow out of that belief, recognising that other people exist in their own right. But the omnipotent traces remain, and the belief that it might still be possible to take back control of the world remains tempting. Most young people have outbursts where, however briefly, they try to take back control of everything because the ordinariness of having to share control with other people feels suddenly too difficult. Levens (1995) writes about the magical thinking involved in eating disorders:

> I have seen numerous paintings made by patients with eating disorders in which they, or some substitute which they recognise to be a symbol of themselves, are sitting on mountain tops, on clouds or in heaven and are looking down at earthlings. (p.9)

Thinking magically, we convince ourselves that we're in complete control. We invent for ourselves hard-and-fast rules or fixed ways of behaving and we stick to them in the belief that they'll allow us to deal with the world entirely on our own terms. Ordinary reality need never impinge.

Counsellors are obliged to fail the fairy godmother test and, when it begins to dawn on young people that ordinariness really *is* the order of the day, counsellors must help them adjust to that ordinariness without the distractions of magical thinking. Eventually young people come back down from their mountain tops to the same old questions, 'How can I be the same as other people yet different? If I'm ordinary, can I still be loveable? Can I be special?'

In the UK, the word 'special' is used by professionals to describe the learning and behavioural needs ('special needs') of those children or young people needing extra help in school. Amongst young people, it's become a term of abuse. 'You're *special...!* He's really *special...!* They're so *special...!*' Of course, their scorn is driven by envy. All young people want the extra attention. They want to be special in some way because, although they may get through school without too much difficulty, it *is* difficult sometimes, it *does* require effort and it *does* feel unfair when their peers get extra help. Like Cinderella, they end up feeling as if everything they do goes unnoticed, although it goes without saying that if they *were* offered some kind of extra help they'd reject it loudly: 'Are you saying I'm special? I'm not *special!*'

They don't say, 'I'd love to be special in some way... Is it too late?' Instead they spend their time – wide-eyed and passionate – idealising or denigrating their rivals. Things are either 'totally awesome' or 'a nightmare'. According to psychoanalytical theory, the need to do this stems from an experience still bubbling away inside from the time when, as babies, we struggle to comprehend two apparently very different mothers – a 'good' one who responds to our needs and a 'bad' one who doesn't (Klein 1957). These mothers come and go in a way that's quite beyond our baby control, leaving us happy and contented or angry and frustrated. The idea that they might actually be one and the same person makes no sense to a baby who can't understand its mother as necessarily flawed, imperfect, doing her best but sometimes making mistakes. So, instead, the baby splits the idea of its mother into the good one and the bad one. *That* makes better sense.

Coming to terms with our mothers (and the world) as a mixture of 'good' and 'bad' probably takes a lifetime. Young people are working away at this all the time – trying to understand, trying to accept their own mixed feelings and, in the meantime, when it's not possible to do that, dividing their experience into the good and the bad. Ruben reckons that his new Drama teacher is absolutely brilliant but the band he saw at the weekend was 'complete shit'. Georgie hates her sister but adores her father's new girlfriend.

Klein (1957) argues that our impulse to idealise is a defence against our fear of being persecuted, a way of trying to convince ourselves, in effect, that the only mother who exists is a good, wonderful one. The more we idealise her, singing the praises of this Best Mother in the World, the more we try to make the bad, persecutory mothers in our heads go away. This may be true but, in my experience, the opposite is also the case: the more we rejoice at the awfulness of everybody and everything, the more we try to convince ourselves that the only mother who existed was a bad one. No good mother ever existed. We never lost her because she was never there in the first place and so we need never feel the pain of her loss. Bettelheim (1976) draws attention to the role of Cinderella's mother in different versions of the fairy tale. Where is she? Why has she abandoned Cinderella? Is she dead? And if she's alive, why doesn't she come and rescue her downtrodden daughter? If Cinderella once had a good mother who was replaced by a wicked step-mother, then whose fault was that?

In their different ways, Marlon and Chelsey are both stuck in Cinderella's kitchen – afraid of being understood, afraid of being interesting, suspecting that their good mother has abandoned them and that a bad replacement is about to punish them… For fierce Marlon and 'I've-got-anger-management' Chelsey, making a relationship with me is like making a relationship with a mother who they assume will be bad and punitive but secretly hope will be good and understanding. For both of them, it means making a relationship with ordinariness where they can retain their prickly sense of difference if they want without forgoing the pleasures of sameness – the consoling pleasures of being understood and interesting.

A Brittle Belief

How then to forgive our flawed mothers, our imperfect parents? How to accept the good things they offer without hankering after all that they can never be? At the suggestion of her family and friends, Lydia comes to see me. She wasn't going to come, she says, because there isn't really a problem and because she has Jesus in her life. She doesn't know what he plans for her but trusts in his goodness.

Psychotherapy has traditionally had an uncomfortable relationship with religion. Jung (1933) took religion seriously, claiming that his patients needed to find 'a religious outlook on life' whereas Freud (1927/2001) referred to 'the fairy tales of religion', describing religious ideas as 'illusions' and 'wish fulfilments'. More recently, Rogers (1961) moved away from the organised religion of his early life to develop a way of helping people based on human values alone. It's rare for me to work with young people who are publicly religious. Those with religious beliefs tend to keep them to themselves and tend, I suspect, to confide in friends who share their beliefs rather than in psychotherapists who might be assumed to be starting from an atheistic or humanistic standpoint.

Hearing Lydia's initial pitch, I might make some traditionally 'psychotherapeutic' assumptions. I might assume that Jesus is her idealised father, helping her avoid the disappointment of the earthly father with whom she's grown up. Or I might assume that Jesus is a particularly resilient or courageous part of Lydia projected elsewhere because she's unconfident about those parts of herself. I might assume that a dogmatic belief system provides her with something to which she can attach, keeping her simple, keeping her safe from ambivalence and ambiguity. I might assume that strict evangelical beliefs protect her from anxieties about sex and death and from her darkest feelings of worthlessness and despair. And I might assume that my psychotherapist's job will be to deconstruct all these beliefs in order to help Lydia face up to some frightening realities.

But this would be to miss the point. Her beliefs make complete sense to her and are probably immensely useful in her life at the moment (Schreurs 2002). Jung (1933) argued that 'religions are systems of healing for psychic illness' (p.278) and, after all, plenty of other people have equivalent systems, equivalent objects of worship and hero-worship, equivalent institutions to which they attach. They hold dear all sorts of things which give solace and meaning to their lives. William James (1902/1985) suggested that religious experience was as 'real' as any objective reality for the person experiencing it and a person might perfectly well have a religious *sensibility* which had nothing whatsoever to do with the theologies and rituals of organised religion. Indeed, argued James, 'any persistent enjoyment may produce the sort of religion which consists in a grateful admiration of the gift of so happy an existence' (p.78). Of more use, therefore, than deconstructing Lydia's beliefs will be trying to understand them in relation to her life as a whole. Any therapeutic relationship begins by trying to understand why a particular belief or symptom has emerged and what role it plays in its owner's life, so I'm curious... Why Jesus? What does Lydia understand 'Jesus' to mean? What might the idea of Jesus resolve for her?

I ask about the people who suggested she come to see me.

'They say I'm not coping,' she says. 'I'm working really hard because I've got exams coming up but they seem to think there's something wrong with that. They reckon I'm not eating enough.'

She's very thin. I ask what she thinks about the things they're saying.

'I am eating,' she says. 'I always have something to eat in the evening but I don't like to sit around talking when I could be getting on with my work.' She says she prays to Jesus to help her with the exams and trusts that he'll take care of her. 'I'm doing it for him. I do everything for him. You probably won't understand that but it's what I believe!'

I hear the rebuke and wonder if I'm just another stupid man in Lydia's life who doesn't understand. Another stupid man... unlike Jesus, perhaps, who understands everything. It seems important to reassure her that I'm actually interested in her beliefs and have no intention of dismissing them. I say something to this effect and add that counselling is a process of trying to understand things together – not a way of getting glib advice or having your beliefs corrected.

She seems pleased with this and keen to carry on talking even though we haven't officially agreed that there's anything to talk about. She tells me about the exams and how hard she has to work simply to do as well as other people. 'When I'm doing my work, I go through everything over and over on my own until I get it clear in my head.'

I wonder whether she's always had to go through things on her own and whether Jesus has therefore become her companion whenever she's feeling fragmented and alone. Guntrip (1968) writes, 'The need of the human being to retain a fundamental sense of organic unity which is at the same time a latent sense of relationship... must have been the core of religious experience all down the ages...' (p.267). But this is psychotherapy thinking and I keep it to myself.

She warms to our conversation. I learn that she has two older sisters, both married with children. She lives with her mother and father but doesn't see much of her father because of his work. Everything's fine at home apparently. She doesn't miss her father because she knows he works very hard and has to travel to earn money for the family. She loves her parents. She loves her nieces and nephews. She has lots of good friends and lots of great teachers.

I feel as if I'm being told – in the nicest possible way – to stop being a stupid man. I ask why she's doing these exams when they require so much work.

'What do you mean?'

'Why are you actually doing them? What's the point?'

'To go to university.'

'And then?'

'Then what? I haven't thought that far ahead. I might do something through my church. There's a scheme where you can go and do missionary work abroad.'

My enquiry was really about the point of anything. Young people may not admit to much religious curiosity but they're usually very much preoccupied with the point of anything (Luxmoore 2000). As I'll describe in Chapter 10, wondering comes easily to them and, from time to time, all young people wonder whether there's something out there greater than themselves. Young or old, we spend time imagining what we could be rather than what we are, writes Dewey (1934, pp.43–52); we then institutionalise this imagining and call it 'religion' – our way of naming a sense of something beyond and better than ourselves, something to which we aspire, an occasional sense of transcendence. Dewey argues that what we call divine is therefore an idealisation of our own best qualities and values. Lydia's Jesus may represent her sense of what's best in Lydia.

'I don't think you can plan too far ahead,' she continues. 'You just have to take life as it comes.'

This is very sensible, but I'm not convinced. It's as if there's something hungry, something unfed about her, determinedly managing on her own, relying on absolutely no one and yet oddly keen for our conversation to continue as if she's secretly hoping for something from me. I'm not convinced by the idea of loving and liking absolutely everybody or by the way she looks me in the eyes, daring me to disbelieve whatever she's saying. She's certainly keen for me to think well of her, even as she keeps her distance, wary of being caught out by some unforeseen therapist's manoeuvre.

When I ask about her family, she wants to talk about her father with whom she's very close, she says, even though she sees him rarely. By the sound of it he can do no wrong. Her mother, on the other hand, sounds more problematic.

'There's not a lot to say about my mum. We get on fine,' she says, apparently lost for anything else to say. 'Mum gets on with her life and I get on with mine. She never went to university or anything like that because she had my sister when she was only eighteen, so she's never had time for a career. She says she wouldn't change anything in her life, though, so she's obviously happy, which is great.'

I ask if Lydia would be happy with her mother's life.

'We're very different, my mum and me. It's great that she's happy with her life but she knows I'm different. She knows I want to do my own thing and she's happy about that.'

'What's she like?'

'What do you mean?'

'Well, what's she like as a mum? What does she look like? What's she interested in?'

Lydia looks irritated, unable to see the point of this. I can only push the conversation so far but I'm curious as to whether there's a relationship between her experience of her mother and her reluctance to eat.

'She's just my mum. She's a bit fat. She doesn't go out much. She likes watching soaps on television… Is that enough?'

I explain, 'It's just that our mothers are always important and the way we end up usually has something to do with our mothers.'

'Not in my case!' she says scornfully. Then catches herself, 'Don't get me wrong. I love my mum!'

Of course you do, I think to myself. But you probably also have feelings which are harder to name about being fed by a fat woman who got pregnant at eighteen, whose husband never comes home and who spends her time watching TV soap operas. I may be jumping to conclusions but there are anorexic girls disgusted by the physicality of food and sex, disgusted by the physicality of their mothers. The way Lydia describes her mother's life makes it sound drab and uninteresting, but if I point this out she'll say that I've misunderstood and immediately insist that the opposite is the case. She can't be publicly critical of anyone, yet there's a mismatch between her words and her feelings. She tells me that her mother's life is interesting, but the way she tells it makes it sound *un*interesting. I may be pushing my hypothesis too far but I wonder if the unconvincing bit is the gap between the world she wishes for ('My mother's great!') and the world she experiences ('My mother's boring!'), between the mother she wants and the mother she gets. I wonder to myself how much it's the ordinariness of her mother that grates and how much Jesus represents a kind of extraordinariness, a transcendence, a way for Lydia to escape from whatever her mother represents and from her own feelings about such a mother.

Another way of escaping might be in relation to food. In many religions, fasting is seen as a way of getting closer to God – master the physical and you'll get closer to the spiritual. I wonder whether not eating means getting closer to Jesus. I wonder whether Jesus feeds Lydia with extraordinary love beyond the understanding of stupid mortals like me and her mother whereas the ordinary, everyday food served up by her mother tastes of dullness, disappointment, submission and shame.

We've started talking about important things without necessarily agreeing that this is what she wants to do. I ask what it feels like talking to a counsellor.

'Not as bad as I thought. You're very experienced and you understand me. I know I can talk to you about things.'

This isn't what I expected. Again, there's a mismatch between 'You understand me' and the suggestion in much of what she's been saying that I don't understand at all. It's true that I don't understand much but Lydia clearly wants to believe that I do. I wonder how much I'm being idealised in the same way as her father. Young people will sometimes say that their counsellor understands when what they really mean is that their counsellor hasn't challenged or contradicted them yet. For these young people, someone who 'understands' is really someone who doesn't exist in his or her own right but is only a narcissistic reflection of the young person. So I'm wary of being someone who 'understands'. I've written elsewhere (Luxmoore 2010) about relationships built on the flattery and idealisation of the counsellor which end prematurely once the idealised counsellor fails to turn everything to gold. In the same way, there are vulnerable young people who embrace religious ideologies only to experience crashing disillusionment when the idealised god fails to deliver world peace and perpetual happiness.

'My friends are really good,' she says, 'and I can talk to them. But there are some things they don't understand, like about my faith and how much it means to me.'

I encourage her to say more.

'It means everything. If I didn't have Jesus, I'd have nothing. I know that he's looking after me all the time. When I'm with everyone in church you can see how happy we are because we all know that he loves us…'

Why has Lydia come to see me? What's she hoping for? There are behavioural ways of helping young people eat more regularly and there are professionals deployed to do this. If we start meeting regularly, I might ask about her eating from time to time and, if she gets thinner, I might eventually need to alert other people. But in the meantime, I can best help by giving her the opportunity to think about the *meaning* of eating very little: the need within her that it expresses or satisfies or makes sense of. Like believing in Jesus, it may be a way of transcending the physical world with all its bodily imperatives. Any presenting problem (such as not eating) will always mask a further problem of how to make sense of ourselves in relation to our parents and the world; how to live with our continuing experience of otherness.

As I described in Chapter 3, there are some babies whose first experience of otherness (discovering what's me and what's not me) fills them with curiosity and confidence. They're happy to go on exploring, intrigued by the possibilities of life. But there are others whose first experience of otherness is terrifying. With its many frustrations and endless negotiations, the world just feels too difficult to bear. Years later, as young people, they're left longing for something to which they can give back control of their lives, longing to be subsumed once more, told what to do and what to think. The imagination of some young people becomes preoccupied with notions of God and the Devil fighting each other – goodies versus baddies. For them, it's as if a primitive story about good mothers and bad mothers (Klein 1957) is being told and re-told.

Freud (1927/2001) argues that 'religious ideas have arisen from the same need as have all other achievements of civilisation: from the necessity of defending oneself against the crushingly superior force of nature' (p.21). I imagine that evangelical religion is the way in which Lydia currently explains to herself the otherness of this potentially crushing world. Religion may be her way of dealing with the extreme feelings evoked in her by relationships with other people – feelings of anger, sadness, hurt, disappointment. Other young people have other ways of dealing with these feelings: they take drugs, join gangs, have babies, fix motorbikes... all ways of trying to make sense of life. I'm sure that institutionalised religion provides a framework for many of Lydia's anxieties, fears, hopes and speculations. But I'm still unclear as to why she's come to see me. Perhaps she senses that she can now manage without all the strictures of evangelical religion, or perhaps she senses that the processes of counselling can provide opportunities for contemplation and enquiry which don't have to conflict with her loyalty to Jesus. Perhaps she senses that there are issues to address which have nothing to do with whether or not she believes in God.

I ask what her parents think about her church-going. 'It doesn't sound like your family's especially religious.'

'They're not! Dad used to go to church when he was young but I don't think Mum's family ever went.'

'Do they mind you going?'

'Not at all! They're fine about it. They can see how much it means to me and how it's affected my life.'

'Like how?'

'It's made me much more confident,' she says. 'I used to get bullied at school when I was younger and because of that I hardly spoke to anyone. Nowadays you can't shut me up!'

'Nowadays you stand up for yourself...'

'Exactly! Because he gives me strength.'

I ask who she'd most like to stand up to in her life.

'That's a weird question. No one! I get on fine with everyone!'

This is the brittle, unconvincing part of Lydia's story. I wonder to myself if it's the part she wants me to help her with, even if she can't ask. When we try to convince ourselves that we *don't* feel angry or disappointed or jealous or afraid and when religious belief suggests that we should always rise above such feelings, it's hard to know how to react when these same feelings continue to bubble away inside us. Guiltily, we try to convince ourselves that they don't exist or we find a way sometimes of punishing our bodies for dragging us down into this emotional maelstrom. In some religions, fasting is seen as punishment, purification. I wonder whether the idea of eating has somehow become connected for Lydia with surrendering to ugly, base feelings. I suspect that my task will be to help her acknowledge her feelings as normal rather than sinful so that she no longer has to maintain the brittle, unconvincing pretence that she's fine and everything's fine and everyone's fine. Hardest but most important of all, I imagine, will be helping her to describe her feelings about her parents.

We agree to meet again, and when the time comes for that meeting, she's late. I wonder if this is a roundabout way of telling me something ('I didn't want to come! I'm disappointed with you!'), but she's full of apologies and offers me an apparently cast-iron, unchallengeable excuse.

'I was doing my Bible study and got carried away!'

It's difficult to challenge young people at the very beginning of sessions. I could suggest that she might have had mixed feelings about coming and her mixed feelings conspired to make her late. I could suggest that she wants me to realise that the Bible is much more important to her than our meeting. She'd deny both suggestions. But sometimes when young people are nervous, their nerves talk through their behaviour: being late is one such behaviour. I think it's normal for a young person to be nervous about meeting with an adult counsellor and so, unless the behaviour becomes habitual, I usually let it go, reserving any challenge until the young person has settled into the session and our relationship has had time to re-establish itself.

She seems more hesitant this week, perhaps having had time to reflect on our first meeting and wary, no doubt, of what we might talk about today. She proceeds to explain to me the importance of Bible study in her life as if, once more, she's checking that I'm not going to attack her beliefs.

I listen. Despite the conviction with which she talks about Bible study, she sounds anxious. I wonder whether the Bible is what she holds on to – literally or metaphorically – when she's feeling anxious. I wait.

'You're quiet today! Are you analysing all this?'

I say that I'm interested in what she's saying because it sounds important to her.

'It is!' she says, pleased. 'Anyway, how are you?'

I say that I'm fine. 'How are you?'

'Fine! Stressed with work as usual but otherwise fine!'

I ask after her family.

'My mum's doing my head in!' Lydia says. 'She keeps coming into my room and trying to help with what I'm doing but she knows absolutely nothing about it. I wish she'd butt out!'

'Do you tell her that?'

'No, of course not! I love my mum. But I still wish she'd butt out!'

'Sounds like it's difficult to tell her what you feel…'

She thinks about this. 'I suppose, in a way… But no one tells their parents everything, do they?'

'Absolutely not,' I assure her. 'We all need our privacy. That doesn't mean we're being dishonest. It just means that we tell different people different things. That's normal.'

For young people and for their parents, this is a vital issue (Luxmoore 2006, 2010). Lydia looks relieved. I find myself thinking about the religious idea of 'confession' with its all-or-nothing implications.

She says that they don't do confession at her church. 'There's no point. It's between me and Jesus. When I pray I tell him things but I know he sees everything anyway so I don't need to spell it out.'

'He knows how you feel about things?'

She nods.

'Including the bad stuff?'

'What bad stuff?'

'Well, there must be some thoughts and feelings that you wish you didn't have.'

She nods ruefully. 'I *really* wish!'

I have to decide. In acknowledging that things aren't always as they seem, she's said a lot, trusted me with a lot. And I'm pleased because we've moved on from her brittle, unconvincing insistence that everything is always fine. It might be better to leave the conversation there and let her assimilate what we've said without pushing her further into actually naming some of the 'bad stuff'.

She continues, 'I'm always wondering what Jesus would say. I know he'd want me to be better than this.'

'I think he'd understand, Lydia. I think he'd know all about feeling angry and feeling disappointed with people.' I remind her about Jesus in a rage turning over the money-lenders' tables, about Jesus upset by Judas's betrayal and about Jesus despairing on the cross. 'He sounds like a man who had some pretty strong feelings!' Jesus the paragon isn't always a helpful idea for young people. In Christianity, ordinariness is important, after all. The story goes that Jesus was extraordinary in that he was the son of God but, at the same time, he was utterly ordinary – born in a stable to a poor couple and growing up as a carpenter. The Christian story is about people being ordinary mortals given an extraordinary purpose by God.

'I didn't know you knew about Jesus!'

'I know enough to know that we're bound to feel bad things about other people,' I say to her, 'and we have to accept that in ourselves. You can call it sinfulness or you can call it people just being people.'

'I call it sinfulness.'

'That's fine. And you can say sorry to Jesus whenever you need to. All I'm saying is that we have to accept that we're bound to have these feelings towards our friends, our sisters, our parents.'

She thinks about this. 'I suppose you're right. I love my mum but she definitely does my head in. I wish she didn't but she does!' She looks as if she wants to say a lot more but stops herself. She smiles.

I smile back.

We've made a start. I'm sure that we'll talk more about her mother, allowing the split between Lydia's love and Lydia's hatred (or scorn or disgust or disappointment) towards her mother to ease, helping Lydia to accept the mother she has as a mixture of qualities and herself as a daughter with mixed feelings. We'll talk about working so hard for the exams and whether that's another way of being as different as possible from her mother. We'll talk about her sisters and the extent to which they've become extensions of her mother in Lydia's mind. And we'll talk about her father whose idealisation rings no more true than her disregard for her mother. Together, we'll digest these conversations – the palatable and the unpalatable.

Lydia's religious beliefs will remain her own. They'll deepen or weaken with time. What matters is that they don't become ways of propping up a brittleness within her which might one day collapse, leaving her feeling that she has no support left. Like most young people in this book, I think she struggles to accept her own ordinariness without denying it, feeling ashamed of it or projecting it onto someone else. At the same time, she probably senses – like most young people – that the world can be extraordinary and she herself sometimes capable of extraordinary things. Dewey (1934) writes, 'The self is always directed toward something beyond itself and so its own unification depends upon the idea of the integration of the shifting scenes of the world into that imaginative totality we call the Universe' (p.19). In calling something 'god', we try to integrate our experience of the ordinary everyday with our occasional glimpses of the extraordinary and transcendent. The idea of 'Jesus' (an ordinary man with an extraordinary purpose) potentially joins up Lydia's sense of the ordinary and the extraordinary in herself.

But this joining-up process doesn't happen quickly or because someone makes a few cognitive resolutions ('I *am* a mixture! I *do* feel bad things sometimes but also I feel good things!'). Living with her parents, she lives with her unconscious tendency to represent them as opposites. Her peace of mind will come when she no longer needs to do this because she's more comfortable with the opposites within herself.

So we'll talk. And talk some more. We'll get used to these ideas so that they become less frightening. We'll get used to a world of overlaps, ambivalences and contradictions – a world in which parts of Lydia disappoint her even as other parts delight.

There's a remarkable passage in Marianne Williamson's (1992) book, *A Return to Love* – a passage frequently misattributed as coming from Nelson Mandela's inaugural speech as president of South Africa. Because the passage speaks to so many young people, encouraging them to be brave, I keep copies nearby and I give Lydia a copy.

She reads it slowly.

> Our deepest fear is not that we are inadequate; our deepest fear is that we are powerful beyond measure. It is our light, not our darkness, that most frightens us. We ask ourselves, who am I to be brilliant, gorgeous, talented and fabulous? Actually, who are you not to be? You are a child of God. Your playing small doesn't serve the world. There is nothing enlightened about shrinking so that other people will not feel insecure around you. We were born to make manifest the glory of God that is within us. It is not just in some of us; it is in everyone. And as we let our own light shine, we unconsciously give people permission to do the same. As we are liberated from our own fear, our presence automatically liberates others. (pp.190–1)

Williamson's words aren't about being exceptional or determinedly different from other people. They're not about everyone being capable of everything. They're simply about becoming the people we can be without being held back by fear. It's the fear that we should be *more* than we can be which makes us shrink in the first place, I think.

'She's right,' Lydia says, looking up, 'but it's hard to do.'

Ordinary Death and Ordinary Sex

It's certainly hard to believe that we're 'brilliant, gorgeous, talented and fabulous' when things keep going wrong, when we feel angry and most alone. A few months after leaving school, with the rest of us back in the classroom and immersed once more in coursework deadlines, Duncan killed himself. Things had been especially difficult in the weeks before his death, but those of us who knew him well knew that his sixteen-year-old life had been difficult long before the events precipitating his suicide. He and I had been talking in counselling for over a year. Others still at school knew him equally well and, like me, knew that he was vulnerable. But we also knew that he was fun and friendly and full of understanding about his life. There are plenty of vulnerable young people in the world after all with appallingly difficult lives: rarely do they kill themselves. So Duncan's death shocked everyone, and after the shock came the recriminations, the sadness and the 'if onlys'. A talented, intelligent, popular boy was dead.

In fact, in the days after his death, he became the *most* talented, *most* intelligent, *most* popular boy everyone had ever known. In our conversations about him, he became extraordinary.

Many of the friends and teachers who'd been fond of him were still at school and so, one afternoon, we held a non-religious event in memory of Duncan with everyone gathered in a large common room around a single burning candle. I invited the people there to speak about him as they wished.

At first, no one spoke. No one knew what to say. This was an unprecedented situation. We were tense. What do you say about someone who's killed himself at sixteen? But then a few people broke the ice and others followed, describing Duncan's many wonderful qualities. We nodded, relieved, agreeing that he'd been an extraordinary friend, student, brother, son. People relaxed, starting to remember and daring to describe his silly moments, his idiosyncrasies, his annoying habits. We laughed. Slowly, Duncan was becoming less extraordinary. In fact, he was becoming downright ordinary again and we were enjoying these tales of someone who was actually like us.

His funeral followed the same pattern. In the church, there were eulogies about what an extraordinary person he'd been. There were reminders from the priest that Duncan was now in the loving hands of God before we left the hallowed stillness and went outside to the banality of the graveyard, to the hole in the ground into which his coffin was lowered. We stood around, watching awkwardly, not knowing the rules, not knowing what to think or how to behave. After all the uplifting eulogies about what an extraordinary boy he'd been, we were faced with damp earth, broken gravestones, cars passing nearby, people needing to pee – the brute physical *ordinariness* of death, the ultimate ordinariness of Duncan.

Death provokes an anxiety about ordinariness. How are we supposed to react to the death of someone we've cared about? Should we take it in our stride? Is death ordinary or extraordinary? In many schools there's panic whenever a student or member of staff dies. Teachers immediately assume that this is something quite beyond their experience and ability to cope, and professionals are hastily summoned from miles away – strangers often with no knowledge of the school or of its community. Implicitly, the message to young people is that death isn't something that ordinary people can be expected to manage. Rather, death requires specialist skills; death is to be feared; death is quite out of the ordinary.

Yet birth and death are the two most ordinary things that will ever happen to us. Everything else may vary but being born and dying are the invariables. So whenever someone's died in a school where I've been working, I've found myself reassuring teachers, saying in effect, 'Look, we can manage! We don't need outside experts. What's happened is really sad and really shocking but we'll be all right. We'll survive. Of course, lots of students will be upset and we'll tell them as much as we know about what's happened. But we'll stay calm. We'll get on with things. We'll be sad when we need to be sad; we'll cry when we need to cry and we'll keep talking to each other. We'll muddle through. Later, we'll go home, do the marking, watch television and go to bed.'

It seems important to be clear with students that death may be very sad but isn't terrifying and needn't overwhelm us. All young people know that they'll die one day and know that their parents will die one day. They think about death a lot: 'What will become of me? Will I die like everyone else or will my life be different somehow? And when I die, will I be remembered? Will my life have been interesting enough to be memorable or will I just cease to exist?' Their problem isn't death but the fact that no one talks about death, which is why sudden deaths like Duncan's are so unnerving. Jacobs (1985) describes death as 'the wounding of our narcissistic pride' (p.65) because the prospect of death reminds us that, despite all our efforts to control the world, to be autonomous, inviolable, absolute lords of all we survey, death will always defeat us. (Suicide is sometimes describes as the last refuge of the narcissist, still keeping control even over the timing and manner of his or her own death.)

Whenever young people mention death or dying, I encourage them to say more because talking with someone about death usually makes the prospect less frightening, less lonely. Because no one will talk about death and because they've therefore been obliged to think about it on their own, most young people take up a firm belief of one sort or another because it's safer that way. Some are absolutely clear: they just *know* that they'll meet their loved ones again. Others are adamant that no such thing is possible. In my experience, it's rare to find a young person who can bear not knowing one way or the other. So in counselling we talk a lot about the person who's dying or who's died and we wonder about those fixed beliefs. Like Duncan, the dead person is initially described as extraordinary – the *most* or the *best* or the *only* – but we keep talking and, inevitably, it's the dead person's humanity that we end up remembering and cherishing – all the ways in which he or she was like us – flawed and mixed-up and kind and sometimes funny.

I think it's the fear of invisibility that really bothers young people, because death sounds like becoming invisible. If we start our lives needing to be noticed and needing to interest our mothers in order to survive, then we probably retain a residual fear of becoming unnoticed and invisible. When we're in a close relationship with another person, we see ourselves reflected in that person's face and know that we exist (Luxmoore 2008). Sex is a huge psychological relief, therefore, because – for a time – someone is most passionately *interested* in us. Good sex offers that affirmation, that wonderful sense of being noticeable and interesting, that heightened sense of existing, whereas bad sex offers an opposite experience. So for young people, when sex begins to feel mechanical, perfunctory…

'It's like we're just *doing it*,' says Bella. 'It doesn't feel like he really loves me. It's more like he just wants to have sex with me. I'll admit it was good the first few times we did it but since then I've stopped caring.'

I ask how she feels after these disappointments.

'Not good,' she says. 'Like I don't matter. Like I'm nothing special. Like he's not really interested in me.'

For Bella, this reminds her of her father's lack of interest and we go on to talk about that, scouting for any sense she may have internalised from her father or from anyone else in her life that she is, in fact, intrinsically interesting. If she can re-connect herself with that sense, then the disappointments of sex may feel less personally damaging.

One of the perennial difficulties for young people is that attracting the sexual interest of another person depends on a body which is changing and over which they have no control. Girls fret about this in public, 'I really hate the way I look! My bum's so big! God, the state of me!' Boys feel just as strongly about their bodies but don't let on. They pretend that everything's fine. Of course, all young people know perfectly well that their bodies will change but no one knows exactly how *theirs* will change – how quickly or how much; whether they'll end up looking big or small, attractive or ugly, 'weird' or 'normal'. They have understandably mixed feelings about their bodies, therefore: on the one hand, it feels good to be growing up but, on the other hand, it's nerve-wracking because these changes are so personal and their bodies make them so vulnerable. 'Anatomy becomes destiny,' observes Coren (1997). 'The body may become not merely an estranged, malign companion, but also a constant reminder of one's abnormality…' (pp.11–14). For young people, it's like starting all over again. As babies, our sense of self develops alongside our sense of our bodies – male or female, tall or small, dark or fair, ugly or beautiful. We learn to talk and walk and, before long, we can begin to take our bodies for granted. But then, at twelve or thirteen, these bodies start changing all over again and we're faced with fresh uncertainty. As Coren says, 'physical changes… have psychological consequences' (p.11). We can hide our feelings but, however much time we put into decorating, displaying or disguising them, we can't hide our bodies. Years ago, running discos, I dreaded having to watch young people arriving in their carefully chosen clothes, their hair perfected, trying to look unconcerned but frantically checking each other out and hoping against hope that they hadn't made some terrible sartorial mistake. One critical or sarcastic comment could smash a person's confidence. It was agonising to watch the fat boy arriving in his expensive black shirt, desperately hoping that no one would mention his weight, or the flat-chested girl running round telling her bosomy friends that their hair looked great.

Young people treat their bodies according to how they feel. Whenever they talk about their bodies, I think they're talking obliquely about other underlying issues like control, dependence and independence, sex and sexuality; issues like what's normal and what isn't.

'Why do I have to look like this?' asks Bella.

'D'you mean, why do I have to grow up?'

'No, everyone has to grow up,' she says. 'I know that. I just don't see why I have to be the one with the crap body. I mean, look at me!'

I want to reassure her.

'I've tried losing weight but it doesn't work. There's nothing I can do about it!'

'And that leaves you feeling helpless…?'

'Yeah, in a way. And it pisses me off! And my mum doesn't help by going on at me about it all the time!'

The way young people feel about their bodies is also related to the way they feel about their parents because, like it or not, our bodies prove that we're something to do with these people. They created us, after all; they're the ones responsible for our physical imperfections and for the unreliability of our changing bodies. So when young people criticise or attack their bodies by starving them, cutting them or stuffing them full of food, they're also attacking their parents, saying in effect, 'Why do I have to go through this? Why can't you make my life easier? It's your fault! How will other people ever be interested in me if I look like this?'

As I described in Chapter 4, the need to be interesting never goes away. There are plenty of young people who take ordinariness as proof of worthlessness and who therefore end relationships as soon as the sexual part no longer seems extraordinary. Perhaps the reason why internet pornography becomes more and more bizarre is because a person gets more and more used to what they're seeing and the ordinariness of that becomes less and less satisfying. Kahr (2007) describes one of the functions of sexual fantasy as the 'avoidance of painful reality'. If our sense of existing as worthwhile people is wobbly, then perhaps extreme sexual practices allow us to feel that we extremely exist.

Certainly, young people struggle to interpret their experience. 'Is my ordinariness a problem or is it inevitable? Do other people feel the same way?' Bella tells me about an uninterested boyfriend who makes her feel uninteresting and we end up talking about her uninterested father. She has to work out whether or not *she's* uninteresting. In the meantime, my non-sexual, continuing interest in her ordinariness supports her, along with the realisation that I don't expect her to come to counselling every week with extraordinary tales simply in order to keep my interest. Ditching an uninterested boyfriend will mean being alone again and it's the aloneness she dreads – being alone with no one to confirm her existence. Winnicott (1965) describes our capacity to be alone as a major developmental achievement because it means separating from our mother having successfully internalised a sense of her which can stay with us wherever we are. We no longer need her to be physically present to confirm our existence. Being able to be alone means being able to bear the prospect of our potential invisibility.

Young people get better at being alone, but, for those persisting in the belief that they should be somehow extraordinary, death punctures that belief, reminding them of their essential ordinariness. A changing body with its unknown sexual possibilities and the brute prospect of death are reminders that childhood is over, that life is finite and that choices are constantly needing to be made.

The Road Not Taken

It's the time of year when I'm having final meetings with a dozen or so of the young people who come to see me for counselling. Some have been coming regularly for two or three years, but we're ending now because they're sixteen years old and about to leave school. We've been counting down the weeks as our ending has approached (Luxmoore 2010) and I've been trying gently to help them think back over their years in school, over all that's happened during that time and the way things have changed. Inevitably, we've also been looking ahead to what might come next.

That part is never entirely clear. In theory, some will leave and start jobs. Some will continue their education elsewhere and over half will come back to school voluntarily. But at this stage of the year, most are still undecided. Whatever they do will depend on their exam results, on what courses are available, on their parents' advice and on how they feel. If they do come back to school, they may choose to start meeting with me again, but, for the time being, this is an ending.

They hesitate. A year ago, many would have claimed to be longing to leave 'this dump', 'this shit school'. But things are no longer so clear. They're intrigued about the future but most will also admit to feeling sad. They say they'll miss school. Some say they wish they could go back to the beginning and start all over again.

I think this moment in their lives heightens a sense that they've had for years – a sense of there being many futures, many lives of which they can live only one. For a few, this will be a relief but, for most, there's a sense of loss and a nagging curiosity about the futures they'll never know, the lives they'll never live. Robert Frost's famous poem 'The Road Not Taken' (1920/2001) captures a dilemma young people live with all the time, an unspoken dilemma at the heart of their hesitation:

> Two roads diverged in a yellow wood,
> And sorry I could not travel both
> And be one traveler, long I stood
> And looked down one as far as I could
> To where it bent in the undergrowth;
>
> Then took the other, as just as fair
> And having perhaps the better claim,
> Because it was grassy and wanted wear;
> Though as for that, the passing there
> Had worn them really about the same,
>
> And both that morning equally lay
> In leaves no step had trodden black
> Oh, I kept the first for another day!
> Yet knowing how way leads on to way,
> I doubted if I should ever come back.
>
> I shall be telling this with a sigh
> Somewhere ages and ages hence:
> Two roads diverged in a wood, and I—
> I took the one less traveled by,
> And that has made all the difference.

It may be that adults have had time to come to terms with the fact that taking one road inevitably involves not taking another, although I suspect that the sense of lost opportunity never entirely goes away: 'I'll never get a chance to try those jobs, meet those people, travel to those places!' It may be that adults have learned to defend themselves against this lingering, protesting sense of loss so that it erupts only rarely in later life as an illicit love affair, as a depressive illness or as a sudden, mid-life change of direction: all ways of expressing the misgivings of adults still agonising, still looking back, still wondering where the other roads might have led.

In school assemblies, in careers interviews, in heart-to-heart conversations with adults who matter, young people are constantly hearing words like 'direction', 'path', 'choice'. They haven't had time and haven't learned how to defend themselves against the anxieties provoked by a road diverging. Their sense of the road not taken is already palpable. 'What if I'd done things differently? What if I'd worked harder at school? Chosen other subjects? Gone to a different school? What if I'd hung around with other people? What if I hadn't met my boyfriend? What if my mum and dad hadn't separated?'

Most of the young people I work with have experienced the separation or divorce of their parents and many have no conscious memory of their fathers (Luxmoore 2006). For all of them, there's an alternative script running in their heads… 'What if my mum hadn't had the affair? What if my dad hadn't drunk so much? What if she hadn't got depressed? What if he hadn't been violent?' There are so many questions, questions, questions, and we wonder together about the alternative storylines. Young people are wondering anyway but wondering about these things *with someone else* makes them feel less troubling. We discover that we don't know the answers but that they're interesting questions. We also discover that not knowing the answers is normal and usually bearable.

Jess doesn't know what her life would have been like if she'd been allowed to stay with her birth-mother. All she knows is that she hates her adoptive parents, feels that she doesn't belong with them and resents their efforts to love her.

It may be that any normal thirteen-year-old would share Jess's feeling, 'I don't belong in my family… I've got nothing in common with my parents… They don't understand me… Other people's parents are different… What if I'd been born into a different family?' but because she's adopted, Jess has always wondered about her birth-mother and about what life would have been like had another 'road' been chosen for her. I think these thoughts have erupted publicly now that she's thirteen because it's safe enough to think about them in the knowledge that, at some level, her adoptive family probably *does* love her, that she *doesn't* have to earn their affection and that she *can*, therefore, afford to rage against what they represent: an autobiographical road that diverged dramatically when she was only four months old. She'll never know the other road or any of the other roads she might have taken.

'I don't know anything about my real mum and they won't tell me! I might have a whole family I don't know about. I might have brothers and sisters…'

I ask what she does know.

'I know that my mum couldn't look after me because she was a drug addict. And I know she's artistic because I've got a letter she wrote to me when I was a baby saying she loves me and she's drawn these little flowers all over it.'

Jess is also artistic and that's the problem. She wonders how much of that artistic talent comes from her birth-mother and, if so, what else of Jess comes from this mother? Her looks? Her temper? Her getting drunk at weekends? So many things might or might not be inherited. Jess has these glimpses of a road not taken for her all those years ago by a team of well-meaning social workers – glimpses of a life unlived. 'It's so unfair. I've asked if I can meet my mum but they say I can't until I'm sixteen!'

We wonder together about her mother, about the circumstances of her birth and about all the things that might or might not have been going on at the time. But her problem is now. She listens to her adoptive parents' advice, to their enthusiasms and attempts to guide her towards a successful life and she wonders, 'Is this really me?' Because she's aware of a genetic road and an adoptive road diverging thirteen years ago, she finds it hard to accept any of their suggestions.

And it's the apparent arbitrariness of that divergence which is particularly hard to take. 'What if I'd gone to other parents? What if they'd been different from Mum and Dad? I could have grown up doing completely different things – I'd be a completely different person!'

There's a film called *Sliding Doors* (Howitt 1998) which follows two parallel narratives with quite different outcomes. One of them follows the main character's story from the moment she catches a subway train. The other follows her from the moment when she misses the train, just failing to squeeze through the sliding doors in time.

By chance, Jess has seen the film. 'It makes you realise,' she says. 'Things like that! The way her whole life turned out different!'

When she's older, Jess will be allowed to trace her birth-mother if she wants. But for now she has to live with a sense of a road not taken, a life she'll never know. For young people who are adopted, this sense is acute because it's more than just a theoretical possibility. Somewhere out there in the world are her birth-mother and father and probably some half-siblings.

For other young people whose parents are separated or divorced the road not taken is often more than just a theoretical possibility: they're obliged to go between parental homes with quite differing cultures. In one home, they can do as they please; in the other, everything requires permission. In one home, they go on foreign holidays; in the other, they don't. In one home, schoolwork is paramount; in the other, it isn't. These young people have to adapt to parents with new partners, with new children, with quite different ways of doing things. So until they're old enough to make their own decisions, it's as if they're required simultaneously to follow two roads with potentially differing outcomes.

April has unfashionable pigtails which make her look younger than her sixteen years. When I mention them, she tells me that she keeps them because she likes them. She's also afraid of the dark, sleeps with the light on and, from time to time in our counselling sessions, sucks her sixteen-year-old thumb.

She lives mainly with her father and hates him for being so strict. But she's equally scathing about her mother who's alcoholic and whom she visits regularly.

We spend the first half of all our conversations discussing the past week's events. Inevitably, they'll have consisted of April putting herself into some tricky situation. One week, she'll have tried a new drug; the next she'll have been to an all-night party; the week after that she'll have been caught shoplifting and the week after that she'll have had sex with someone else's boyfriend.

I think she actually brings me the same dilemma every week, a dilemma constantly running through her head because, in a sense, all these stories are about her parents. They're all versions of *I know I shouldn't have done it but I did* – a juxtaposition of her father's strictness ('I know I shouldn't have done it…') with her mother's carelessness ('…but I did'). April's road has diverged and she's still at the junction, unable to make up her mind which route to take and so making forays down both routes: should she be like her father or like her mother? They split up when she was six and, in a way, it's a six-year-old girl who visits me every week: a girl with pigtails, a fear of the dark and a thumb-sucking habit.

It would be tempting for her to choose one road for the sake of it – to become a harsh disciplinarian like her father or a louche libertine like her mother because the divergence between them is hard to contain. So we try to make sense of two very different kinds of people – how they met, what might have attracted them to each other, what the early years might have been like when April was born and growing up. I suggest that her experience – although difficult – is rich and that she'll emerge eventually as a resilient person.

But she's having none of that glib counsellor stuff. 'I hate my life!' she says. 'I hate seeing my mum when she's in a state and I hate my dad when he's shouting at me all the time!'

We keep talking because that's all we can do. The more we talk and the more April can keep thinking about these opposites within the containment of a counselling relationship, the more she can find a way of living with them, taking for herself some of her father's strictness, perhaps, and some of her mother's ability to live for the moment. They're parts of any young person, after all. And April has other parts: a shy part and a loud part; a baby part and a grown-up part; an organised part and a chaotic part… The more she can think and talk about these divergences, the more she can contain them within herself without automatically externalising or enacting them recklessly at her own and other people's expense.

'I *like* getting drunk,' she tells me. 'I like going out and having fun with my friends. And most of the time my dad doesn't even know because I say I'm staying over at Charlotte's.'

'What would he say if he did know?'

'He'd go mad. He hates me drinking. But I like it!'

'Your mum drinks…'

'I know. But she's an alcoholic. I'd never get that bad.'

I say nothing.

'I know my dad only wants the best for me but I've got to have some fun, haven't I!'

And so we go on. April knows that I think drinking is fine in moderation so this conversation isn't about drawing a moral line: it's about getting used to the conflict inside her and learning to live with it. Freud (1915/2001) writes: 'When two wishful impulses whose aims must appear to us incompatible become simultaneously active, the two impulses do not diminish each other or cancel each other out, but combine to form an intermediate aim, a compromise…' (p.186). In my experience of young people, this compromise is difficult. For any young person, holding together such opposites is a developmental achievement: 'I can be shy and I can be loud! I can feel like a baby sometimes and like a grown-up at other times! I can be organised and I can make a mess of things…!'

Unsurprisingly, young people find it impossible to go down two different roads at the same time. Some refuse, choosing one road (one household, one part of themselves) or behaving in such a way that the choice is made for them ('Your dad says he doesn't want you coming over to his house any more if you're going to behave like that!'), because, for many, it feels like having two identities. They long for a single identity ('Part of me wishes that they'd get back together although I know they never will!'), a straightforward road. Once upon a time they thought they were on that straightforward road and then suddenly one day after weeks of rows and silences and late-night conversations going on downstairs it was announced that the road was diverging, 'We've decided it's better if we split up.'

Susan always smiles, always says hello and, when I stop to talk with her and her friends in the corridor, is always asking me cheerfully about counselling and why I'm a counsellor and what do people talk about in counselling. Then, typically, something else pops into her head, she apologises and dashes off with her friends in attendance.

Oddly, I don't see her for several months until a teacher contacts me to say that Susan's apparently 'in meltdown'. Days later, Susan stops me in the car park and asks for an appointment.

When we meet, she looks different. Less make-up than I remember, slower to smile and much more guarded. She starts to cry. During the last year, her father's new girlfriend has had a baby, her sister's left home and her best friend's moved to another part of the country. In addition, she's had glandular fever and has got important exams starting in two months' time. She isn't sleeping and has started having panic attacks.

There are young people like Susan who set off gaily down one particular road, learning one particular way of dealing with life, only to meet with a dead end. The road narrows and narrows; that particular way of dealing with things becomes more and more limiting until the young person has to turn back, in effect. Susan agrees with me that people have always seen her as happy, positive, enthusiastic...

'And I *am*!' she says, 'It's just...'

'Just?'

'I don't know!'

'Just that I can't keep being like that? Just that people don't realise what I'm really like?'

'Yeah!'

She can't continue down the happy, smiling road any longer. In the last year, she's suffered all these changes in her life with a Susan-laugh and a Susan-smile and she can't keep going on like that. Now, for the first time in her life, she *has* to start being sad and angry and helpless and overwhelmed, even though that's not what people expect of smiling Susan. And she has to learn to share these parts of herself with other people, which is why the safety of our counselling room is a good place to start.

I tell her this and suggest that she has panic attacks because her life is panicking and wants to escape.

She seems to understand.

Hayden is similar. Apparently he's stopped coming to school and can barely get out of bed, crying for no obvious reason. According to his family, he's always been a very positive person, but now he's telling them that everything's pointless, everything feels too much and he's not himself.

His doctor has said that Hayden's depressed. She's prescribed medication and has sensibly suggested that he talks to the counsellor in school.

But getting him to my counselling room is difficult. When we meet eventually, I learn that he's been bribed: his mother has actually promised him money to come and see what counselling is like.

'You really didn't want to come, Hayden!'

He shakes his head. 'Don't take this the wrong way but I never thought I'd be someone going for counselling. I know other people come and I haven't got a problem with that. I just never thought it would be me! I'm not that kind of person.'

I ask what kind of person he is.

He says he's good at basketball. His father used to be a professional and has encouraged him to be good but now Hayden's smoking cannabis and drinking, not training so hard and not playing so well. His father's disappointed and the two of them have been arguing a lot. 'My dad really pisses me off! Some days I just feel like walking off the court and telling him to fuck off in front of everyone!'

'But you haven't?'

'Not yet, I haven't. I feel like it, though!'

I ask what would happen.

'Don't know...' His eyes glaze with tears and I can almost feel him forcing himself not to cry in front of another man. He seems cowed. With all his strength, he holds the tears back and manages to change the subject, talking about his friends. He's got lots of them, he says. They go out drinking. They have a laugh. He wants to get back to the way things used to be, before all this started, before it got too much. 'I don't know what's wrong with me!'

His tears have gone. He looks at me for the answer and I don't have one. In fact, I've been wondering whether his depression is the best thing that could have happened to him because it sounds as if his former self had become unsustainable – all that testosterone, all that manly banter, all that basketball to please his father. I've been wondering whether becoming depressed is, in effect, a last-ditch attempt to say 'Fuck off! I'm not like you think I am and it's about time you noticed!' Listening to him talk about his family, it sounds as if vulnerability and doubt aren't tolerated and are certainly not modelled by his father ('He says I should get on with my life, says there's no use worrying...'). Hayden's mother – the person who bribed him to come to counselling – may well be a different matter. She may represent softer qualities struggling to emerge in a family where getting on with your life is what counts and where crying is for girls.

Surprisingly – given all that he's said about male friends – the only people he can really talk to are girls, he says. 'I don't know why. They just seem to understand better.'

I think Hayden's gone as far down the macho road as he can and has reached a dead end. There's nothing wrong with basketball, nothing wrong with having lots of male friends and nothing whatsoever wrong with being macho as long as those things don't imprison a person. And I think they've imprisoned Hayden. The contrast between his macho self and crying self suggests that the two parts have grown miles apart.

One way of describing the situation is to say that, for him, the choice is between going down a road called 'Father' and a road called 'Mother'. For him, the Father road is familiar and narrow and frustrating while the Mother road is unknown and tearful and embarrassing. And because they veer off in such different directions, it's hard to decide which road to take. Lots of other young people struggle with the same unconscious dilemma: young people adopted and uncertain whether to identify with their adoptive parents or with their original birth parents; young people living with a step-parent and unclear how much to abide by the step-parent's rules; young people going between two parental homes with quite different expectations. 'Who am I? What am I supposed to be like?' It's a painful dilemma to live with unless, like Hayden, you block it out by concentrating on one possibility alone. Until that becomes intolerable.

He agrees that he's always been a 'daddy's boy', enjoying the same things as his dad and pouring scorn on boys not interested in basketball, football, boxing, fishing. 'Most of the time I'm really close to my dad,' he concedes. 'I don't talk to my mum all that much. She's not interested in the things me and dad like doing.'

I ask what she's like.

'Don't know, really. Like any mum, I suppose… Never really thought about it!'

Thinking about it will be where we start – thinking about the vulnerabilities he's suppressed, the dependent feelings he's squashed, the longing he's turned into scorn. Choosing between a Father road and a Mother road is impossible: we have to find some way of identifying with or, at least, making sense of them both, however flawed their parenting and however unreliable their behaviour might have been in the past. Even when young people have never even *met* their fathers, they have to incorporate an idea of that man into an evolving sense of themselves (Luxmoore 2006).

In my experience, young people can't rest until both Mother and Father roads have been explored. So Hayden and I talk about his mother and about what she represents. He begins to relax a little. We talk about his father and mother *as a couple* – how they met, what attracted them to each other, what stories are told in the family about his birth, who gave him his name, what he knows or imagines about the first years of his life… Putting his parents back together as a couple is like putting two parts of Hayden back together. We wonder about what two people who seem so different nowadays had in common when they first met, what they loved (and possibly still love) about each other, how they complement each other and how Hayden, as their son, is actually made up of both his parents – macho *and* vulnerable, boyish *and* dependent. He has to find a way of acknowledging the shortcomings of his parents without losing sight of what they've given him in their very different ways.

Delmore Schwartz's famous short story *In Dreams Begin Responsibilities* describes a young man sitting in a darkened cinema and, by some surrealistic chance, he's watching a film of his parents' courtship long before he was ever born. The film follows their movements on the day his father ended up proposing to his mother.

At one point, the young man watching bursts into tears and is comforted by the woman in a nearby seat. A little later, he can't bear to watch the film any longer as his mother accepts his father's proposal of marriage. He stands and shouts, 'Don't do it. It's not too late to change your minds, both of you. Nothing good will come of it, only remorse, hatred, scandal, and two children whose characters are monstrous' (Schwartz 2003, p.6). The young man is silenced by an usher and finally, after another outburst, is ejected from his seat by the usher who scolds him, 'What are *you* doing? Don't you know that you can't do whatever you want to do...?' (p.8). Continuing to berate him, the usher drags the young man from the cinema into 'the cold light', warning him, 'You will be sorry if you do not do what you should do, you can't carry on like this, it is not right, you will find that out soon enough, everything you do matters too much...' (p.9).

We're conditioned by the choices other people make for us long before we're able to make choices for ourselves. Those choices may constrain us in some ways but they also provide a necessary structure to our lives. I think Schwartz is describing the grief young people feel about the road not taken, 'What if I could turn back the clock? What if my parents had never met? What if other choices had been made? What if things had been different...?' The usher represents a necessary pragmatism, 'How can I accept the way things are? How do I take responsibility for the imperfect, ordinary, inevitable and sometimes dull reality of my life?'

What Is and What If

Fraser finds it hard to accept the dull reality of life. Like Jess in the last chapter, he's adopted and shares a fascination with the life he's never lived. He currently lives in a conventional, suburban home with two parents and a sister who's also adopted.

'My parents are so boring!' he moans. 'They don't understand anything about what I want to do!'

Because he likes making things, they want him to be an apprentice carpenter, whereas Fraser wants to be a set designer for theatres and rock concerts. He tells me how well-connected he is with local theatres and music venues, how keen they are for him to work for them and how easy that will be once he's left 'this shitty school'.

He exaggerates, but I think exaggeration is partly a way of exploring the road not taken for him – wondering, in effect, 'What if I were to escape from my adoptive parents and suburban anonymity? What if I'm secretly destined to do something exotic, glamorous, extraordinary?'

He holds on to the idea of becoming a set designer for all he's worth, insisting that there will soon be a choice of jobs waiting for him in the world of theatre. But closer to home, things keep going wrong. He keeps falling out with other students at school. Whenever there's a new production or some special occasion requiring a set, he's always part of the crew, but every time we meet he tells me yet another story about the unfair way in which he's being treated, about how much his hard work behind the scenes is being overlooked *yet again*, about how much people are taking him for granted and about how fed up he's feeling. He's always going to resign, 'Then they'll realise! Then they'll have no one left who understands how the whole thing works!'

It's as if Fraser compulsively joins families (the set designers, stage crew, lighting crew, backstage crew…) only to become disillusioned once they don't live up to his expectations, once he can no longer bear their otherness. But as soon as this happens, there's always some new opportunity around the corner, some new family to be joined and, as a fall-back, there's always the idealised family of professional theatre designers waiting to welcome him at the first opportunity.

His story is always the same. It's about being valuable but rejected, deserving but unappreciated. It's a story about a road he sees up ahead at the school-leaving junction which will definitely, *definitely* be better than the one along which he's forced to trudge at the moment. Whatever its variations, I think it's a story about trying to understand his adoption. 'Why me? Why wasn't I wanted? What if I met up with my birth-mother one day? What if there's a wonderful family waiting for me out there somewhere?' I think Fraser is forever telling two birth-mother narratives. In one, she turns out to be fantastic; in the other, she's terribly disappointing.

I could suggest to him that his birth-mother – fantastic or disappointing – is in the past and it's the present that matters, the mother he has *now*. That would be true but would ignore the fact that that Fraser has an unconscious mind like everyone else and things from the past *unconsciously* affect our lives now whether we like it or not. It's never as simple as 'forget the past'. Until he can find some way of accommodating two very different birth-mother stories, the present will never be just 'the present'.

The term 'surplus reality' (Blomkvist and Rutzel 1994) is used in Psychodrama psychotherapy to describe all the things that haven't happened to us – the things we didn't say, the relationships we didn't have, the dreams which didn't come true. These things are as much part of our 'reality' as those things which did happen. They're our regrets, our aspirations, our many 'what ifs' and, like

Fraser, they affect us powerfully – haunting, taunting, confusing, frustrating us… So, far from encouraging people to stick with a narrower sense of daily reality, trying to manage the art of the possible, Psychodrama makes a virtue out of surplus reality, allowing people to explore those 'what ifs' in a group setting, to experience what it would have been like to meet the grandfather who died when they were small, to speak with their mother when she was a young woman, to receive a round of applause from the people who matter or to say the things that needed to be said but were impossible to say at the time. This is done in Psychodrama by inviting the group member to *be* their own grandfather or their own mother as a young woman. This isn't self-indulgent wish-fulfilment because these people and conversations already exist in our heads: they're already real in that sense and they really affect us even though we've never met them or experienced them or had the chance to say them. They're all roads not travelled.

The young man in Delmore Schwartz's cinema (see p.92) can't bear his sense of 'what if', spontaneously shouting out and getting ejected by the usher as a result. 'What a ridiculous waste of time!' the usher might be saying to the young man in exactly the way that a frustrated parent might beseech a son or daughter not to get carried away with life as it *might be* but to concentrate on life as it *is*. Freud (1911/2001) describes our primitive, unconscious wish for satisfaction as 'the pleasure principle'. Gradually, he argues, the pleasure principle comes up against the frustrations and limitations of external life and has to do battle with 'the reality principle'. We spend our time (young people like Fraser spend *a lot* of time) engaged in 'reality-testing' until, eventually, we find some way of accommodating our needs within our particular circumstances. Freud proposes that 'people turn away from reality because they find it unbearable – either the whole or part of it' (p.218). So the pragmatic Freudian usher might insist that the young man isn't doing himself any favours by thinking about things which can never and will never happen.

I don't think it's that simple. The proponent of Psychodrama, Jacob Moreno, claimed to have reproached Freud, saying, 'You analysed [people's] dreams, I try to give them courage to dream again' (Marineau 1989, pp.30–1). For Moreno, giving people back their dreams and fantasies meant giving them back an important part of their mental health ('what if') without taking away their ability to live pragmatically and deal with the otherness of the world ('what is').

Fraser's birth-mother exists powerfully in his unconscious imagination (he speaks about her obliquely in recurring stories), so I encourage him to talk to her in surplus reality, *as if* they were actually meeting, bringing together his sense of 'what if' and 'what is'.

'What would you say to her?'

'I'd want to know why she decided not to keep me.'

'And what d'you imagine she'd say?'

'Don't know, really. That she was too young? Or too fucked up?'

'She might have had mixed feelings…'

He sighs. 'I suppose so. But then why didn't she have an abortion if she knew she wasn't going to be able to look after a kid?'

We pause.

I ask him what his mother would say to that.

'I suppose she might have been scared,' he says. 'Might have thought she couldn't cope. Might have just wanted to get attention for having a baby…'

'She sounds pretty normal, Fraser…'

He shrugs. 'Maybe.'

'If you met her, what would you want her to know about your life?'

'That it's been hard,' he says immediately, his face reddening. 'That it's hard not knowing who your parents are.'

'And that you've done okay?'

'Yeah,' he says. 'I mean, I'm not blaming her or anything. She probably did what she thought was best.'

'But it's been hard for you…'

'Yeah, it has.'

In a Psychodrama group, this imaginary scene with his mother would be enacted using another member of the group but with Fraser swapping roles – asking his mother a question and then becoming his mother in order to answer it. In effect, we'd be enacting a conversation already going on in his head – giving it a voice and, crucially, giving him the experience of becoming his own mother. From that experience and from a therapist's careful questioning of Fraser and his mother, it might become possible for him to experience his mother as a mixture – neither ordinarily bad (like the teams he complains about at school) nor extraordinarily good (like the idealised teams waiting for him in professional theatres), but a mixture.

In counselling, a similar process can happen without needing to be physically enacted. As we talk together, imagining the conversation between Fraser and his mother, I think he begins to develop a sense of her *from her point of view* as well as from his own. All we're doing is wondering about her, but wondering is vital. A good listener doesn't have to be forever formulating the next penetrating question or wise pronouncement. Sometimes a gently floated comment which begins, 'I wonder…' is enough. It's neither a question nor a pronouncement but a way of thinking aloud, a way of inviting without necessarily expecting a response from the other person, looking at things from different angles, speculating and imagining without necessarily clutching at answers, 'I wonder what that felt like… I wonder why she said it… I wonder what he meant… I wonder what they were thinking…' With nervous or inarticulate young people, 'I wonder…' is particularly helpful because the young person doesn't feel obliged to come up with an answer.

Wondering comes naturally to young people in any case. Sometimes it's called 'daydreaming'; sometimes it's called 'being in a bad mood', 'needing some space' or 'listening to music in my room'. But really it means wondering – drifting into a reverie, working things out, imagining what life would be like… if only, 'If only I was popular… If only my parents were together… If only I was clever… If only people understood… If only things were different…' Young people's sense of 'if only' is constant, persisting as the sense of an alternative life, a life they could have ended up living... if only.

The early events of Robyn's life are shocking and what remains of her family is now dispersed around the country with people in prison and out of contact with each other. Yet every December she describes to me a scene in which the whole family is sitting around the Christmas table with a big turkey ready to eat, all wearing paper hats, all laughing and having fun.

She's never had this experience in her life. It's not a memory from the past. Rather, it's an 'if only' dream of a life where people are kind and funny and pleased to see each other. Perhaps it's an image from television or from a novel or from hearing her friends talk about their lives in which scenes like this really do happen.

If only... She can't let go of it. Every time she tells me about the family around the Christmas table she cries, looking at me and asking, 'Why can't my life be like that? Why do I have to be the one with the shit life?'

There are young people like Robyn who can conjure an image like this seemingly from nowhere and, as her counsellor, I'm left wondering what to do with it. Should I be cruel to be kind, making it clear that this will never happen and that she should therefore stop torturing herself? Or should I encourage her to believe that this dream might be possible one day as long as she doesn't give up on it? Together we wonder about the past, about why things happened the way they did, about what caused people to be like that. We stretch her story this way and that like dough, assimilating all sorts of motives and possibilities. And we wonder about her future, about the things she plans and the things that might get in the way. The likelihood is that Robyn's future life will be neither as bad as it's been in the past nor as good as she hopes. What I'm doing is helping her to integrate her 'what is' story with her 'what if' (or 'if only') story. We're constructing a story about ordinariness with which she can bear to live. But this is difficult. Balindt (1968) describes the way 'the patient repeats over and over again that he has been let down, that nothing in the world can ever be worth while unless something that was taken away or withheld from him – usually something unattainable in the present – is restored to him' (p.89). Robyn has never had the experience of being around the Christmas table with her family, so where exactly does her dream come from?

A Promised Land

The idea of a promised land to which they'll escape one day is central to the experience of young people. It's an idealised land, for sure. But however disastrous their lives may have been, all young people can describe an equivalent scene, 'I'm by a lake, watching the sun go down with my dad... Me and Mum are on an amazing holiday together... Our whole family is back together for the first time and we're having a barbecue... I'm in the crowd on the day we win the championship... I meet up with my gran and she's no longer dead and we talk about what happened...' Bollas (1987) describes these longings as 'psychic prayers'. In my experience, young people have an almost instinctive sense of this promised land always tantalisingly out of reach. In *The Wizard of Oz*, it's to be found 'somewhere over the rainbow'. In *West Side Story*, it's 'a place for us'. Again and again in the songs of Bruce Springsteen, it's an innocence which might one day be recovered.

When small children demand that everybody should stop arguing and just be friends, when they insist on a world in which everyone loves everyone else, we applaud them, delighting in their innocent utopias, their peaceable kingdoms. How lovely! How cute! But when as inarticulate, embarrassed, bad-tempered young people they argue against war, when they insist that equality and justice *are* possible and that the world *can* be a better place, we say that they're being ridiculously idealistic and we laugh at them.

Perhaps young people find it possible to be so idealistic and to dream of a promised land – not because they haven't suffered at the 'school of hard knocks' or been to the 'university of life' – but because they're closer to an experience adults have forgotten. Plato believed that adult knowledge was merely a matter of remembering explicitly all that we knew implicitly when we were children. In the Platonic tradition (Newsome 1974), Wordsworth admired children 'trailing clouds of glory' because he saw children as necessarily closer to the source of all things wonderful, to 'the glory and the dream', to a half-remembered heaven from which the child had recently come (Arnold 1879).

Perhaps young people's sense of a promised land refers back to some original experience of mothering, of reverie, of relaxed, reflective mutuality between a mother and her baby – what Meltzer and Harris Williams (1988) call 'aesthetic reciprocity' – an experience going back, even before birth, to a balmy, symbiotic womb of 'oceanic feeling' (Freud 1930). Perhaps it's what Bollas (1987) describes as 'an existential recollection of the time when communicating took place primarily through the illusion of deep rapport of subject and object' (p.32). Perhaps our sense of a promised land encourages in us a sense of our own perfectibility which (for Lydia in Chapter 7) becomes a religious possibility, a perfection called Jesus. Perhaps, perhaps...

I suspect that Robyn, whom I described in the last chapter, gets her image of the family around the Christmas table (her promised land) from before she was born, because by all accounts she experienced none of that blissful maternal accompaniment after being born: her mother left immediately and only came back into her life when Robyn was three years old. But it may be that other people took her mother's place and Robyn unconsciously remembers a quality of *their* care which, years later, emerges as her Christmas table image.

Images of a promised land abound in most cultures. Christians propose that there was once a wonderful garden in Eden. They tell of a promised land offered to Moses by God. According to Hesiod, in Greek mythology there was once a time of perpetual, unconditional nurture and this was 'The Golden Age' where peace and harmony prevailed and no one had to work because everything was provided in abundance. People were noble, wise, beneficent, enjoying a land of milk and honey. (Robyn's image is of people being fed.)

Nussbaum (2001) argues that the idea of a golden age unconsciously reminds us of 'the omnipotence of the infant, its sense that the world revolves around its needs, and is fully arranged to meet its needs...' (p.185). It's a world in which the infant is still undifferentiated from its mother, enjoying her unconditional, limitless love. As a myth, The Golden Age complements Jung's (1972) idea of an unconscious, residual, archetypal 'mother' to be found deep in our psyches and in so much of the religious and secular symbolism surrounding us. Jung argues that it's not our birth-mothers who affect us so powerfully but an unconscious, much more primitive sense of mothering which those birth-mothers come to embody. This idea isn't so different from Plato's and Wordsworth's descriptions of the child emerging fresh from a celestial home or from Nussbaum's suggestion that this idea of an original home or golden age really describes a primitive experience of maternal containment in which our needs are always met.

Although it emerges from no conscious memory, Robyn's Christmas table image is of abundant mothering. It represents an experience she feels she's lost or been denied ('Why can't my life be like that? Why do I have to be the one with the shit life?'). Bollas (1987) describes the way adults continue searching for a quality of transformational mothering 'in order to surrender to it as a medium that alters the self' (p.14). If we could only find that promised maternal land our lives would be easier and our cares would vanish. He goes on, '...all children store the quality of an experience that's beyond comprehension... There is a wish that some day that which is beyond knowing will eventually be known' (p.246). So we seek experiences which make us feel good about ourselves, the way we felt in the very beginning when we were most closely attached to our mothers. Perhaps the kind of drug-taking which searches for a blissful release from worldly cares is another attempt to find a promised land making everything all right; an attempt to recreate a womb-like safety, merging back into an original maternal presence, no longer beset by anxieties of otherness. I wonder how much young people's frustration and rage erupts because the world won't be the way they want it to be and won't be the way they feel it *should* be. Instead that world insists on being disappointing and imperfect when what young people demand (and seem almost to remember) is perfection. Phillips (1998) writes, 'Rage becomes the often forlorn hope of reinstating a damaged ideal version of ourselves' (p.102).

In response to the loss of her promised land, Robyn switches between desperation and hopefulness. Sometimes I meet with her and everything's going wrong, 'Why do I have to be the one with the shit life? Why does my family have to be so fucked up? Why do bad things keep happening to me?' At other times, I meet with a girl who's excited about new friendships and wants to show me her latest poem ('It's my best!'); a girl who just *knows* that everything's going to be better from now on.

She talks a lot about her friends, always looking to recreate a version of her Christmas table image through them. They promise so much but disappoint most of the time. Robyn worries whether that's her fault but usually concludes that, no, it's their fault. Some young people automatically blame themselves whenever things go wrong while others automatically blame other people. So accepting that responsibility is shared with other people and letting go of our old omnipotent fantasies ('I'm everything! I'm all that exists!') is a developmental achievement. The belief we once had in our own perfection may be lost, but we retain a residual trace of what Freud (1914) calls the 'ego-ideal', an unconscious memory of how things used to be back in the beginning when we were still merged with a maternal world, still undifferentiated and wonderful. Freud distinguishes between this ego-ideal and the 'super-ego' – that other internalised, insistent, punitive voice forever telling us that we should be more than we are. Exposed to the voice of the super-ego, our memory of perfection (the ego-ideal) becomes uncomfortable because it reminds us not only of a perfection we've lost but, according to the super-ego, a perfection we must now recover.

Kohut (1971) develops this idea, arguing that, as we gradually become aware of our own limitations, like Robyn we invest our lost sense of perfection (Freud's ego-ideal) in other people. They become the idealised parts of ourselves to which we now keenly attach. However, when anyone or anything that we've idealised in this way fails to live up to our expectations – the way Robyn's friends fail to live up to hers – the danger is that we experience this failure as persecutory, as if we've been deliberately let down. We're left wishing to be associated with things extraordinary, wonderful and perfect but, at the same time, we're wary of the power of such things to disappoint, hurt and confound us, like Robyn – always disappointed with her friendships.

Her dilemma is whether to settle for a world of chaotic, transient relationships – a world she knows only too well – or hold out for the promise of happy Christmas table scenes and reliable relationships in the future. In some ways, her life would be easier if her Christmas table image didn't exist, because then she wouldn't have to suffer the pain of not having (or no longer having) that experience. But I think her life would also be impoverished because her sense of a promised land means that she doesn't give up but carries on looking for something more reliable and rewarding than the chaos currently surrounding her life.

As the epigraph at the front of this book suggests, she's glimpsed a promised land and is haunted by that, as if she's been separated from it, as if it's been taken away. Professionals sometimes speak about young people and separation as if separation was a straightforward process: 'He just needs to separate... She's having trouble separating... They're about to separate...' but I wonder about the extent to which we *ever* entirely separate from anyone or anything. Do we ever really give up on our childhood idealism or merely cover it with layers of protective cynicism? Do we ever entirely forget what we once felt? Do we ever 'get over it'? Winnicott (1971) argues, 'It could be said that with human beings there can be no separation, only a threat of separation' (p.108).

Separated from the Christmas table scene she imagines, Robyn lives with its loss and with a series of unresolved questions: 'To what extent am I responsible for what's happened to my family? Because I'm capable of hating as well as loving, how much has my hating ruined everything? Is my otherness too much? Am I too weird?' She senses that there's a mothering out there somewhere which is loving and kind but – like Cinderella – can't help wondering why it's been denied her and whether it's her fault.

There are young people who never get beyond the unfairness of this loss and remain inconsolable, believing themselves to have been picked on by some uniquely malevolent fate. 'Why, oh why has this happened and why does it keep happening to me?' But how does anyone come to terms with an original, formative experience of separation, with the loss of a promised land? How do we come to accept it as (more or less) inevitable, as 'ordinary' and not as the persecutory experience it seems to be? How can our brief glimpse of a promised land support us in our attempts to make loving relationships with other people without feeling endlessly denied and cheated? How can Robyn transform her sense of loss into something more useful than just a perpetual, yearning, debilitating sadness? Jung (1972) writes, 'Our task is not, therefore, to deny the archetype, but to dissolve the projections, in order to restore their contents to the individual who has involuntarily lost them by projecting them outside himself' (p.18). As she continues her journey, making choices about which road to take, how can Robyn keep her Christmas table image inside herself as something to sustain her rather than as something perpetually lacking in her life?

A Disillusioning

Though we may search for a better world, a better life out there somewhere, our past will always be with us. Bollas (1987) argues that we invest in the promised lands of a new job, a move to another country, a holiday, a change of relationship and:

> The search for such an experience may generate hope, even a sense of confidence and vision, but although it seems to be grounded in the future tense, in finding something in the future to transform the present, it is an object-seeking that recurrently enacts a pre-verbal ego memory. (p.16)

In other words, our promised lands are memories of a time long gone. So if we're like Robyn in Chapters 10 and 11 and always searching in the future for something from the past, to what extent do we remain imprisoned by those past experiences, obliged endlessly to search for them only to re-experience the loss of them? To what extent can new experiences ever be transformational?

Some young people react to the apparent loss of their promised land by hating all that it represents (Luxmoore 2010). That way, its loss can't hurt them because (they claim) they never wanted it in the first place. Others deny that a better world could ever be possible and appear bewildered that anyone could suggest such a stupid idea.

It would be easy for Robyn to defend herself in these ways but she doesn't. I remember another young person – Omar – defending himself resolutely against anything hopeful or well-intentioned. According to Omar, things always went wrong because people were always out to get him. One day he came home from school and saw a 'For Sale' sign outside the family house. He concluded immediately that no one had bothered to tell him that the house was being sold because no one cared about him. He couldn't countenance the possibility that his parents might have forgotten to tell him or that they'd meant to tell him but the sign had gone up prematurely or that, in their fighting with each other, they'd thought it kinder not to worry him with the prospect of yet another major disruption to his life.

Omar was in the process of losing the family life he'd known and I felt sorry for him. It was hard for him to consider that the appearance of the 'For Sale' sign might possibly have been a mistake because, for him, mistakes meant that people weren't in control. Conspiracies, on the other hand, meant that they *were* in control, because everything in a conspiracy was necessarily planned and plotted: nothing happened by accident. Omar preferred to believe in conspiracies, in things always being under someone's control, and yet, interestingly, couldn't and wouldn't take control of his own life. He didn't want to go to school, but nor did he want to go to the work experience arranged for him as an alternative. He complained that working in a supermarket was beneath him and working in an office too difficult. So he sat at home, doing nothing, rejecting his mother's offers of help but persisting in the belief that she *should* nevertheless be sorting things out for him because she was his mother and therefore able to control everything. It seemed as if he was walking along the road of his life, head down, terribly hurt by what had happened to his family, refusing to look up at the possibilities stretching out ahead and hoping against hope that he'd never arrive at the place where the road diverged and he had to make a choice, his life reduced to a single organising statement, 'No one cares about me!'

What counsellors call 'organising statements' are summaries of our lives condensed into a single phrase or sentence, so that underneath everything – underneath all the stories, the feelings, the relationships – our lives come down to one simplified statement and that's our autobiography in a nutshell, *that's* how we see the world.

I remember introducing myself to another boy, Nathan, explaining about counselling and asking him to tell me a bit about himself.

'I've got ADHD.'

It was the first thing he said – nothing about his family or about how he got on at school or about whatever caused him to make this appointment – just 'I've got ADHD'. Translated, his 'I've got ADHD' statement might have meant 'There's something wrong with me' or 'I'm different from everyone else'. He began to talk and it became clear that he'd organised his whole life around the belief that there was something wrong or different about him so approached every situation and every relationship on that basis.

Louise was different. She didn't come straight out with it (most people don't) but I was listening for some sort of organising statement during our first session as we moved from talking about school to talking about her family. With five minutes left, we started to talk about when she was younger and I asked about when she was born.

'I wasn't wanted.'

We hold on tightly to these organising statements. They evolve over the years, helping us to make a simplified sense of the world. So *that's* why things go wrong, Louise might conclude; *that's* why people treat me as they do: it's all because I was never wanted in the first place.

Because these statements make so much sense to their owners, they're very hard to shift. Trying to convince Nathan that there was nothing fundamentally wrong with him would have been a pointless task – water off a duck's back. Beliefs like that don't change overnight. If I'd tried to convince Louise that she *was* wanted because lots of people liked her (which they did) and probably loved her as well, she'd have laughed and thought I was a complete idiot. All I could do was wonder with her about the circumstances of her birth – her parents' relationship, getting pregnant, what was happening in their lives at the time, who was around when she was born, what they might have been feeling and whether their feelings might have been a little mixed... What we were doing was gently going over the beginnings of her life again, wondering together, potentially loosening some of her entrenched beliefs and allowing – crucially – for the possibility that important people in her life might have had mixed feelings. She might have been an inconvenience to her parents in some ways and adored by them in others. We didn't come to any conclusions. We just wondered.

Young people hold on to different organising statements of which the most common is 'It's not fair!' No amount of trying to convince a young person that, really, it *is* fair makes any difference. To that young person, the whole world is unfair; life's unfair; this school's unfair; these rules are unfair; teachers are unfair; what happened this morning was unfair...

This default belief hasn't emerged overnight so trying to change it through sensible, rational explanation won't work. Usually, it's a belief which starts for all of us when we're babies: it's unfair that my mother's around sometimes and not at others; it's unfair that I have to share her with my siblings; it's unfair that I can't control the world; it's unfair when I get hurt... 'Why do I have to be the one with the shit life?' asks Robyn. For young people, being able to share with someone their frustration, anger and despair at life's unfairness (without being given well-meaning advice) helps. Talking about where that deep sense of unfairness comes from also helps, and for professionals it helps to know that the vehemence with which a young person says 'It's not fair!' usually comes from a lifetime of believing it.

Young people don't say 'It's unfair that my promised land has been taken away from me' (it would be a strange thing to say!) but it's what they mean. Balindt (1968) writes about his patients, 'Over and over they repeat that they feel let down, that nothing in the world can ever be worth while unless something they were deprived of is restored to them' (pp.88–9) and, until that time, they'll be worth nothing. Omar and I talked about the unfairness of the 'For Sale' sign appearing and how much it hurt.

We spent time remembering the old days when family life seemed straightforward. We talked about what was good then which could never be taken away. Those good memories had stayed with him and it was important that Omar took them with him into the next stage of his life to set against the feeling that everything was conspiring against him.

Robyn believes that she's never had an experience of her promised land because she's never *actually* sat around the Christmas table having fun with a re-united family. And yet, as I've argued, she wouldn't have been able to conjure up such a vivid image and feel it so powerfully if she'd never had some equivalent experience. Whether from archetypal, ante-natal, infantile or from some long-forgotten social experience, Robyn got her image from somewhere.

'Why do I have to be the one with the shit life? I think about my friends and their families and I've got nothing like that!'

When she's feeling like this, it's pointless to disagree. In effect, she's saying, 'It's unfair that my promised land has been taken away from me!' She has a brother she likes and some good friends but – objectively – she's right. Compared to some people, her life isn't as full of Christmas table scenes. So how to acknowledge that objective reality while allowing Robyn to enjoy her image and feel enriched by it?

I ask her to tell me more about the Christmas she imagines.

'Why?'

'Because I'm curious and because I want to understand more about what it means for you.'

'It means that my life's crap!'

'Your life is certainly different from a lot of people's,' I say. 'Tell me about the scene you imagine.'

She tuts and seems embarrassed. 'It's nothing really. Just people in my family getting on together and not arguing.'

'And it's Christmas?'

'Yeah! Because I love Christmas! I love everything about Christmas. And it would be good if everyone was there.'

I ask what would be happening.

'I don't know! We'd probably be opening presents and – I don't care what presents I've got – I'd just love to be there with everyone opening theirs. And we'd all be joking and stuff. And we'd have silly presents, too. You know – useless things that don't cost much but they're a laugh!'

'Like?'

'I don't know. Like a thong for my dad or those sunglasses that you can use to drink through like a straw!' She smiles. 'And we'd be playing Christmas songs and singing along and all having a drink and then a big meal.'

'Turkey?'

'Eugh! I hate turkey! But, yeah, turkey and roast veg and wine and speeches…'

'Speeches?'

'Yeah, you've got to have speeches! And everyone has to make one because it's more fun that way.'

'What would you say in yours?'

'I don't know.' Her eyes well up. 'Actually, I'd probably cry.'

'Because you'd be happy? Because you'd be sad?'

'Both, really. I'd be happy that we were all together and sad that it's never actually happened.'

We pause.

'It's happened in your heart, Robyn.'

She sighs. 'Just hasn't happened in real life, though, has it!'

'No, it hasn't.'

'Well,' she smiles, 'I'll just have to hope, won't I!'

We both smile.

Robyn's version of a promised land is particular to her but other young people have other promised lands waiting somewhere over the rainbow. They dream of going to university, of finding a particularly wonderful boyfriend or girlfriend, of achieving some spectacular success… All these dreams can be understood in relation to an unconscious, half-remembered mothering experience now seemingly lost. Going to university might represent something about acceptance or being recognised as good enough; finding a wonderful girlfriend or boyfriend might mean being loveable; achieving success might mean being special or worth something...

For some young people, a counselling service (and the possibility of getting to know a counsellor) represents another promised land in which a certain kind of mothering experience might be on offer. Yet counselling services (at least in schools) have a chequered history. In some schools they're well-established and admired while, in others, their history is uneven and their existence precarious. Some schools resort to using peripatetic, external counselling services, claiming that young people would never feel safe talking to an existing member of the school staff. Of course, funding and personnel issues are important factors in schools, but there's also an unconscious level at which young people's (and teachers') transference to a school counselling service and to the *idea* of a counselling service will be to some kind of mothering-figure. The status of the counselling service within the school – geographically and culturally – will always say something about how the students and staff feel towards mothers and mothering. Are mothers to be welcomed or to be avoided at all costs? Are they trustworthy? Should they play a central part in our lives or remain peripheral? ('Please don't come into school, Mum!') Given their inevitable imperfections, can mothering-figures ever be of help to young people and professionals?

Adolescence involves a changing relationship with our external and internalised mothers. We still need them as badly as ever – that much never changes – but the way we express that need changes radically. There are degrees of independence, intimacy and privacy to be re-negotiated. To keep counselling out of a school is to suggest that this awkward, ambivalent but potentially reparative process (Luxmoore 2010) is too hot to handle, too shameful, too childlike. Robyn will strike up relationships with her teachers and these relationships will also have mother-and-child undertones whereby she feels more or less recognised, more or less valued. Meeting by arrangement with a school counsellor, she simply engages more formally with these processes. I think she keeps coming to counselling because she senses that something useful might be on offer – an experience of otherness neither punitive nor utopian, a promised land provoking all the usual expectations but this time *moderated* – neither as good as she hoped nor as bad as she feared. In counselling, I'm aiming to disillusion young people – not catastrophically because that would only frighten them – but gradually. I can't protect them from the outside world, but we can talk about it; I can't prolong our relationship when it's ending, but we can be honest about what it's meant to us; I can't guarantee that things will go smoothly in the future, but we can wonder together about what the future will hold.

Winnicott (1965) argues that a baby first experiences its mother as an illusion wherein baby and mother are merged in mutual delight and service. A good-enough mother, he argues, will gradually disillusion her baby, a little at a time, helping the baby to bear degrees of frustration, disappointment, solitude. If the disillusioning process is too fast, the baby will be unable to cope and will defend itself with narcissistic grandiosity, refusing to enter into a relationship with otherness. But on the other hand, if the process is too slow, the baby will never learn to bear the realities of otherness – of relationships which can be unfair, unpredictable, neglectful, infuriating. For this disillusioning or separating process to happen, the mother 'plays' with her baby in what Winnicott (1971) calls a 'potential' or 'intermediate' space. Disillusioning can take place safely and gradually as the baby learns the limits of its power, getting used to its mother's separate existence and learning to bear the frustrations of sharing power with her.

The knowledge that there are adult responsibilities waiting for them just around the corner causes young people to re-visit this original disillusioning, separating process (Blos 1962). They panic like babies. And then calm down. They blame 'school' for everything. And then relax. They lash out at the people they love. And then say sorry. As the end of school approaches, they experience an erratic disillusioning at the hands of the maternal institution. Sometimes she goes much too fast ('Teachers keep on and on at us about the bloody exams!') and sometimes too slowly ('We've got the exams in six weeks and we haven't even started the last module yet!'). Either way, young people always complain that the pace isn't right.

I need Robyn to enjoy the illusion of our connectedness before arriving at the disillusioning knowledge that we're actually two quite separate people. I need her *then* to find a way of living with the satisfactions and dissatisfactions of what two quite separate people can offer each other. Because there's a sense in which her Christmas table is an image of *our* relationship – abundant perhaps, tantalising for sure but always out of reach. We end up smiling and appreciating each other, knowing that our relationship can be no more and no less than that – a smile of recognition, an acceptance of the other person's otherness. Her relationship with me is transitional, easing her journey from babyhood to adulthood, from Balindt's harmonious interpenetrating mix-up to a world of otherness, surprise and separation. A world of ordinariness.

As any parent or parent-figure knows, that journey will be fraught with difficulties: 'I can't stand your constant mood swings! It's ridiculous! These days we never know how you're going to react!' It's often said that young people's moods go up and down because their hormones go up and down and I'm sure that's true. But young people's moods also change because their lives are changing and because moods give them time to think.

In moods, young people withdraw and take stock. When something important is happening or has just happened, moods press the pause button. By 'going into one' as young people say, they buy time to think about the ways in which they've just been thwarted, opposed or disappointed. They stomp off upstairs or storm out of the house, saying, 'I'm not listening to this! You're doing my head in!' Then, once they're safely in a mood, they can begin to get used to the situation; they can begin to adapt and decide how best to deal with other people being so annoying; they can decide how to deal with their own mixed feelings about the situation. Bollas (1987) argues that 'in a mood, a part of the individual's total self withdraws into a generative autistic state so that a complex internal task is allowed time and space to work itself through' (p.100). Moods are useful because they protect young people and protect *other* people *from* young people. Moods also serve to remind other people that the young person has an inner life – a life full of feelings which are hard to talk about because, in moods, young people regress. 'Go away! I don't want to talk about it!' Of course, young people can then be accused of being childish and irresponsible; and rightly so, because, in a mood, young people usually go back a few years and *do* feel childish – full of vengeance, impotence, sadness, regret. Typically, they lose their grown-up ability to talk about things. 'Just leave me alone!' But moods are always communications – ways of trying to say something important which can't be said in words – and as communications they need to be understood.

'I'm in a really bad mood!' says Gemma, sitting down.

I ask her to say more.

'My dad's really pissing me off. At the weekend, right, I asked him if I could go back to Stacey's house after the party and he said that was all right. So I told Stacey I was coming back to hers and then he goes and says he never said it and I've got to go straight home after the party!'

I say nothing, waiting. Every week I hear about the real or imagined inconsistencies of parents. Every week young people tell me about their bad moods and how unfairly they've been treated. Every week I listen, waiting until the outburst subsides and we start to talk about what's underneath – in this case, Gemma's feeling that her father loves her younger sister ('She's allowed to do anything!') more than he loves Gemma and her feeling that he disapproves of her now that she's started talking to boys, now that she's no longer his little girl. Moods, argues Bollas (1987), are intended to 'conserve something that was but is no longer' (p.110). When the world feels too difficult, when the responsibilities and complexities of grown-up life feel too great, young people retreat into moods. Then, when they've had time to adapt, they re-emerge ready to carry on with the difficult task of growing up. Gemma's life is changing. Things are no longer straightforward. People are contradictory.

At the school where I work, I write a monthly column for the parents' newsletter. As Christmas approached one year, I wrote the following:

DISAPPOINTMENT

In the weeks leading up to Christmas, I listen to lots of young people telling me about the presents they're going to get, the people they're going to see, the things they're going to do at Christmas. I hear about Christmases when they were small and how they couldn't wait for the day to come.

With all its nostalgia and expectation, looking backwards and looking forwards, Christmas raises an important issue for young people. Why does the exciting world that I remember seem so disappointing nowadays? Why are my presents no longer as surprising as they were? Why are people so irritating? Why do our family routines seem so predictable?

Adolescence can feel like the bad hangover after a heavy bout of childhood. Everything nowadays seems tired, dreary, aching, dull and, above all, disappointing.

Learning to live with disappointment is one of the hardest tasks of growing up and, once childhood ends, Christmas is always about being disappointed. One way in which young people deal with this is by saying that they hate Christmas, hate their presents and hate everyone in their family. That way, they try to preserve the idea of a wonderful, exciting Christmas which they feel is now somehow being denied to them. Coming to terms with the inevitable disappointment of Christmas takes time because it's really about coming to terms with the disappointment of life itself now that we're adults. How can we look forward to something and enjoy it when it's imperfect? That takes some getting used to.

I know these columns get read by parents and by students at the school because they tell me so but I usually get little response to the actual content of what I've written. This time it was different. I heard from several parents that they thought this piece was 'depressing' and 'pessimistic'. Interestingly, I heard nothing from any students, and I think that was probably because they recognised their experience in what I'd written whereas their parents, trying hard to make Christmas happy and enjoyable, found it 'depressing' to be reminded that their loving efforts would only ever be partially successful. I had no desire to undermine anyone's Christmas. My point was that it takes young people time to get used to Christmas as an inevitable mixture of hope and disappointment. The danger for sons and daughters is that, if something isn't wonderful, they easily conclude that it must be terrible. At Christmas time, all sorts of family rows erupt which are really about our inability to bear hope and disappointment as two sides of the same experience. So when a family grows older and things are no longer the way they used to be, when a counselling service fails to live up to the idealised expectations of it, when a counsellor fails to live up to young people's expectations, when I fail to live up to Robyn's expectations of me, that's when the real work begins: the work of gentle, kindly disillusionment, keeping hold of what's good and possible in a relationship while acknowledging what's not.

That's when a middle ground called ordinariness begins to emerge.

Back to the Garden

Letting go of an illusion of perfection, there's a sense in which young people are always dealing with loss: the loss of an original mothering presence, the loss of a promised land, the loss of the possibility of ever being an Olympic champion, the loss of so many roads not travelled. In this sense, adolescence is about adaptation and renewal, about finding something to compensate for these losses.

Zoe describes her old and new life in terms of gardens. In the old garden there was space to play with her mum and dad and brother and, although the garden was small and rather overgrown, she liked it. Now that her parents have split up, the garden in the new house is much bigger than the old garden, and her mum's boyfriend is working hard to sort it all out, cutting everything back and planting in neat rows. No one's allowed to go in until he's finished, but Zoe says she hates this garden and wouldn't want to go in anyway.

Mention gardens to young people and their associations are immediate – having and not having a garden, wanting a garden, hiding in gardens, stealing from gardens, throwing stuff into gardens, wrecking gardens… When they're small, many children relish having their own patch of earth in which to grow things, and horticulture is often used to help rehabilitate emotionally damaged young people. Clearly, gardens mean something.

Sometimes I tell young people the story of Frances Hodgson Burnett's *The Secret Garden* (1911/1987) because it's about the loss of an emotional as well as a physical garden. When her parents die, ten-year-old Mary is emotionally and physically alone, *entirely* alone, unloved and unloving. She's sent to live at the country house of an uncle who's been avoiding all relationships since the death of his wife. Because this man can't bear to be reminded of his wife, he goes away for weeks on end, leaving a young son, Colin, shut up indoors, apparently disabled and apparently dying. Both Colin and Mary are physically alone and emotionally starved.

However, a kind of promised land is waiting out on the moors and inside a secret, walled garden near the house. This garden is locked up, overgrown and dying of neglect ever since the death of Colin's mother, who apparently loved to spend time there. No one has been allowed to go into it since the day she died.

Mary goes out and plays on the moor, feels better and, by chance, discovers the key to the secret garden buried in earth near the locked door. She sneaks inside and, later, invites Colin to join her.

Unofficial therapists are available to help the two children. One of these is fourteen-year-old Dickon who embodies all the emotional and physical health that the moor represents. Another is Dickon's mother who supplies the children with 'food'. Encouraged by Dickon and his mother, Mary and Colin begin to tend the secret garden and the secret garden tends them. Hodgson Burnett writes: '…the secret garden was coming alive and the two children were coming alive with it' (p.290). Having both been outsiders, knowing only difference, they begin to discover the excitement and comfort of relationship, connection, community. From the garden they receive the kind of mothering both have lacked. It's 'a kind of magic,' observes Colin, which 'if you keep thinking about it and calling it perhaps it will come. Perhaps that is the first baby way to get it' (p.244).

Whenever I tell my simplified version of this story to young people, they're entranced – and not because of my story-telling skills! Most know nothing of moors or walled gardens or country houses with gardeners and servants. But something seems to touch them. I think it's the abiding image of a beautiful garden wasting away; an image of a kind of mothering they dream of re-discovering: a mothering which contains them safely while they play and is invigorated by their presence. The young people listening to me aren't orphaned but they know what it's like to feel alone where once upon a time they felt attached. They know what it's like to have lost a metaphorical garden and to feel adrift, separate, longing to re-discover that garden and perpetually looking for the 'key'.

Like Zoe and her two very different gardens, young people invariably speak of loss when they speak of gardens. Their sense of loss is focused on many things but particularly on the idea of a garden as some kind of 'home'. In counselling, they end up talking about 'home' because how young people feel about 'home' is an indicator of how they feel deep down about life generally: 'I might be getting chucked out of home... I just want to go home... No one at home seems to care... I love being at home... Everyone at home keeps having a go at me... I don't get to spend enough time at home...'

We're always nostalgic about 'home'. Even if we've never really had one, we still seem to know what we mean. Some people would say that this is because our first home was a warm womb and that we never entirely lose our unconscious memory of that place; that in fact we spend our lives longing for it and trying to recreate it, getting worried when it's not there or when it seems to have changed in some way. It's as if we have an external home (a house lived in by a family) as well as an internal home (a sense of belonging and mattering). So when young people are talking about 'home' they're sometimes talking about important family members and sometimes they're talking about a deeper sense of feeling whole or feeling fragmented. The distinction usually gets blurred.

'How are things at home?'

'Terrible! My mum and dad are arguing all the time. My gran's not well and my sister's totally doing my head in. In fact, my life's a complete mess!'

'Because of your family?'

'No, not just because of them. To be honest, I've been feeling like it for ages. I try to work hard at school but then I think, "What's the point?" And sometimes it's like you can really trust people but then they let you down. I don't know. It's confusing... Soon as I'm sixteen I'm leaving home and getting a flat!'

Young people are always insisting that they're about to leave home and live in the mythical 'flat'. But soon the reality of the housing market dawns and they patch things up at home. Most find some way adapting to other people's expectations of them now that they're older and find some way of living with the inevitable imperfections of 'home'.

'There are days when I just want to forget everything and go and get drunk but I know that's pointless because there are things I really want to do with my life...'

We keep talking, trying to make sense of these competing voices, getting used to the idea of a 'home' with different kinds of people inside, some of whom argue and compete with each other but all of whom represent 'home'. Writing about refugees, Papadopoulos (2002) points out that 'home' is usually associated with homecoming, whereas refugees have no home to which they can return and therefore have to establish a new sense of what home can mean. I think this is also true of most young people (albeit in less dreadful circumstances) as they venture forth into the world. Like refugees, they must learn to adapt and adapt again to an ever-changing sense of home.

But that's hard. With every loss comes the feeling of powerlessness, of having been unable to prevent some important event or change from happening, hence every young person's fantasy that 'If only I was different! If only I was powerful – powerful like a superhero, a magician, a god!' And yet power is something about which young people are decidedly ambivalent. At home they oscillate between 'Just tell me what to do!' and 'You can't tell me what to do!'

Perhaps the moment at which we become 'adults' is when we can bear to experience power and powerlessness simultaneously as a kind of ordinariness, a mutuality. Young people practise this sharing of power in counselling, taking the initiative themselves sometimes and sometimes letting the counsellor take the initiative; choosing what to talk about and when to talk about it. Sharing power isn't easy. A young person might stop coming to see me because my power to understand seems frightening. Another young person might stop coming because I'm clearly powerless to make his life better. Another might stop coming because I insist on sharing power with him rather than letting him dominate our conversation. But most young people do keep coming back and keep practising this sharing of power.

There's an opportunity to practise at the end of every session. I'm meeting for the first time with seventeen-year-old Samina who's frozen at a point in her life where two roads diverge: she can't decide whether to go to university or to get a job working in her father's shop. She's afraid of both options and the deadline for making a decision is fast approaching.

She's painfully shy, giving all her power to me, initiating nothing and constantly struggling to articulate what she's trying to say, resorting usually to a pained, 'I don't know…'

We struggle through until it's almost time to finish and, because I don't book young people for a fixed number of sessions, we need to decide what happens next.

I ask, 'Shall we meet again?'

'If you want…'

'What do you want, Samina?'

'I don't mind.'

I say it's important that she decides.

She winces. 'I don't know…'

With some young people, I make the decision for them if I think that, at this stage in our relationship, they need the experience of someone else taking responsibility and knowing what's best. Other young people might need the experience of taking at least some responsibility, some power for themselves.

'I know it's hard,' I say to her, 'but it's also important that you decide because there are lots of things in your life where other people have made decisions and you *haven't* had a chance to say what you think.'

'Yes,' she agrees, 'but I really don't know…'

'Well we could meet next week and see how it goes or we could leave it for now and not make another appointment.'

Again, she twists uncomfortably. 'I don't know…'

When a young person is genuinely stuck, there's a risk that my insistence will provoke them into making any decision just for the sake of it. So I put a spin on things. 'It seems like we've made a good start but I know there are lots of things that we haven't had time to talk about yet… I suggest we meet again. What do you think?'

There's a long pause before she reluctantly answers, 'Maybe… meet again?'

'You sure?'

'If that's okay?'

For Samina, this is important. Like so many young people, her 'home' life was affected by her parents' fighting and drinking. She kept quiet during those long years, afraid of making things worse, hoping that things would get better. But they didn't, and I think the experience took away a lot of her confidence, leaving her with the feeling of powerlessness which she brings to counselling.

A few weeks later, the deadline for university applications passes without her consciously making a decision one way or the other, although allowing the deadline to pass is effectively a decision to stay at home and work with her father. But that really doesn't matter: she can always apply to university next year. For now, she's exploring something more important which will inform all her decisions in the future – what it's like to be in a relationship in which she *isn't* powerless. In this relationship, she can begin to make decisions about what we do and don't talk about and can begin to transfer that confidence into the rest of her life, including her 'home' life.

As the weeks go by, she talks more readily. She dresses more stylishly. She remembers and tells me things spontaneously – laughing sometimes. And when we get to the end of each session and I ask about meeting the following week, she smiles and says, 'Yes.'

As I've said, all young people live with losses of one sort or another. Most adapt and survive, finding new sources of comfort and strength, finding new relationships with friends, lovers, parents and professionals: relationships which allow them better to balance sameness and difference and enjoy the ordinariness of life. Some aren't so lucky. Because ordinary life with its constant balancing feels impossible, they cling to a dream of extraordinariness and sometimes enact that dream with disastrous results.

There are adults struggling in exactly the same ways…

Ordinary Parents, Ordinary Professionals

Snow falls and freezes. Roads become treacherous. Schools decide to stay shut and, hearing the news, young people gleefully go off snowballing. They hope that the snow lasts for ever and that their school stays shut for as long as possible.

The recriminations start almost immediately. Parents complain that there wasn't enough snow to warrant their school staying shut. They themselves managed to get to work despite the condition of the roads. They protest on local radio shows and email their school pointing out that a school closing is very inconvenient at home (which it is) and that schoolwork always suffers (which it does).

But whatever the rights and wrongs of a school's decision to close because of snow, I think that our adult reaction is partly informed by envy. After all, we can't go snowballing any more. (We wish we could!) Nowadays we're too busy and tired and stiff for all that. We can't take days off work. (We wish we could!) We can't waste time. We can't be irresponsible. We can't afford to get behind with our work.

We live with our lost childhoods. Snow may bring the issue into the open, but I think our envy of young people is there all the time. Of course, it's not the *only* thing we feel – we love our children and we want them to be happy – but we envy them as well. That's hard to acknowledge because it feels vaguely shameful, but it's a feeling which subtly informs our relationships with young people.

Dom, for example, says that his parents hate it when he goes out with friends on Friday and Saturday nights, drinking, having fun and messing around with girls. 'We don't do anything bad. It's just mucking about. But they're always having a go at me about it and threatening to take my phone away.'

I ask what he knows about his parents' childhoods.

'My dad's dad was really strict – I mean, *really*! He wouldn't let my dad do anything! And my mum was at boarding school most of the time.'

I'm sure that Dom's parents are only trying to protect their son from harm but, at the same time, it must be strange for them, thinking back to their own childhoods and comparing their teenage lives with his.

Livvy tells me that she wants to be a professional dancer but that her mum thinks it's a stupid idea. 'My mum left school when she was sixteen and started working in the shop and apart from when she had me and my brothers she's been there ever since. They've just made her Assistant Manager.'

Again, I'm sure that Livvy's mum is trying to be realistic about professional dancing – not wanting her daughter to be left empty-handed if the dancing dream doesn't come true. But at the same time, I'd love to ask Mrs Canning about her own teenage dreams, about what her parents expected of her and whether she was ever allowed to experience the sensuality and excitement of dancing.

Young people's potential to be different (having unruly fun on Friday nights, becoming a professional dancer) fills adults with mixed feelings: we're pleased for them but also resentful and envious of them. For young people, it's hard to know how to interpret a parent's reaction. 'If they love me like they say, how come they're so strict with me? They say they want the best for me but all they do is stop me doing things!'

Helen's struggling. She's her parents' only child and seems not to be what they want. When her school grades are poor, she's not allowed out for several weeks. When rumours circulate locally about her friends, she's not allowed to see them. When she dresses up to look sexy, she's made to change her clothes. She says that she's thought about running away several times but would only end up coming home and being grounded by her parents *for ever*.

With her understandable desire to be independent, the danger is that Helen will end up doing something dramatic and irreversible in order to break free from her parents – getting pregnant or getting expelled from school, for example. I imagine that her parents are being especially protective of her because she's their only child, but it turns out that both parents have children by previous relationships and their relationships with these children are difficult. Her mother has three grown-up children she hasn't seen for five years and her father has two daughters from another relationship, both of whom are extremely hostile towards him.

Given this, it sounds as if she's become her parents' project, '*This time* we'll get it right! *This time* we'll prove that we're good parents by producing an obedient, loving, respectable daughter!' I feel sorry for Helen but sympathise with her parents' need to prove themselves. We talk about their lives. Helen agrees that she may be getting caught up in things which are not entirely about her and that the situation at home may not be as personal as it feels. The thought seems to reassure her.

I suggest that, whatever happens in the next few years, she'll be fine because she's independent and thoughtful and sensible and good fun.

Her eyes glisten with tears. She may have been fighting them for a long time but it's as if she's believed her parents' criticisms, 'You can't be trusted, Helen! You always let us down, Helen! You'll come to no good, Helen!' Hearing someone she respects say 'You'll be fine, Helen' clearly touches something.

There are other young people programmed to achieve all that their parents never achieved ('You'll be exceptional, even if we never were!'). Teachers are forever complaining about parents who believe that their child is a genius and that his or her poor marks are simply down to bad teaching. There are parents who despise their own ordinariness and so there are sons and daughters who live in fear that *their* ordinariness will be unacceptable to their parents. They carefully address their cards to 'The Very Best Mum and Dad in the World!' because the thought of being an ordinary, good-enough, flawed mum or dad clearly isn't acceptable for some mothers and fathers.

From time to time, I'm contacted by parents anxious about a son or daughter and hoping that I'll have the answer. When we meet, they're anxious to know whether their experience is typical. 'Are we a family like any other or are we different? Is our child's behaviour normal? Is our family normal?' When they talk about their son or daughter, they're often talking obliquely about parts of themselves with which they're struggling – parts of themselves they'd like to change or erase, parts which let them down, show them in a bad light or make them seem stupid. For some parents ordinariness is a relief, while for others it's a curse. They wish they could be different. They wish they weren't condemned to ordinariness by their disobedient son or daughter.

Just as parents and young people bring to counselling a continuing conversation about ordinariness, teachers struggle with the same anxieties. Kamila comes to see me because she can't decide whether or not to give up teaching. 'I really like the students,' she says, 'but I don't like it when they misbehave, and my head of department has told me that apparently my classroom management skills aren't good enough and I'll never get promoted until I can learn to keep the whole class quiet. But the trouble is that I don't *want* them to be quiet! I want them to enjoy the lessons and have fun. I don't want them to see me as some kind of dragon! That's not the kind of teacher I want to be!' Kamila relies on reason and kindness to persuade her students to do as they're told, but the more she reasons with them the more they seem to misbehave. 'Maybe I'm not cut out to be a teacher,' she says, frowning. 'I spend all my weekends doing stuff for school. I don't have a social life any longer because I'm thinking about school all the time. And it makes no difference! They don't take any notice!'

Apparently, she grew up wanting to be a dancer but put on weight and gave up that ambition. Then, during university, she fell in love with a married man who eventually went back to his wife, leaving Kamila to graduate with no plans, having invested all her hopes in this man and his promises of a life together. She drifted from job to job before deciding to train as a teacher.

'What do you think I should do?' she asks.

There are counsellors who are horrified that I see staff as well as students for counselling. There must be 'boundary problems', they say, because it's impossible to have a professional working relationship with a colleague whom you're also seeing for counselling. I think this is unnecessarily purist. The needs of teachers are just as pressing as those of students; an unhappy teacher is just as problematic for a school as an unhappy student. The fact that we can have both kinds of relationship at once helps to make counselling normal and ordinary – not freaky or shameful or debilitating. We keep the two relationships separate, and I explain from the outset that when we see each other in the staffroom or corridor I won't stop and ask about the things we've discussed in counselling – not because I'm uninterested or not wondering how things are going but because it wouldn't be fair to re-start that conversation with other people around and without time to talk properly. I say the same thing to students whom I'm also bound to encounter in other contexts.

'You're the counsellor,' says Kamila. 'What do you think I should do?'

She's twenty-eight and relatively new to teaching. It's often assumed that staff using the school counselling service will be young or new to teaching like Kamila. This isn't so. I see teachers nearing retirement who are worried about what the future will hold and wondering whether it's all been worthwhile; I see administrative staff feeling marginalised and undervalued *yet again* in their lives; I see teachers who are lonely, who are in unsatisfactory relationships or who are struggling to work with difficult colleagues; I see canteen staff looking after sick relatives, teaching assistants hating their jobs... The important thing is that the school counselling service exists for everyone, regardless of their age or status. I happen to work in schools, but I think the same facility should be available to professionals working with young people in any other context. Kamila might easily have chosen to train in social work or youth justice or psychology or youth work – her personal needs would still be affecting her professional work and her dilemma with young people would still be the same... 'How do I manage to be both firm and kind? How do I support a young person emotionally while enforcing the rules and being prepared to insist on them when necessary?'

'Should I quit teaching?'

I ask what her parents would say.

'Huh, my father would say it was my fault! He'd say, if you can't stand the heat, get out of the kitchen! But he's got no idea what teaching's like. He thinks you just tell people to shut up and they do!'

She hasn't actually discussed the situation with either of her parents. As she talks, they emerge as harsh and disciplinarian, pushing their daughter to succeed academically at the expense of friendships and fun. 'I was never going to be a dancer as far as they were concerned,' Kamila says. 'I was supposed to be a doctor or a lawyer or something they could be proud of.'

'Not a teacher?'

'Not unless I was going to be the headteacher! And that's not me. That's not what I'm interested in doing. I want to help the students!'

There's always some connection between choosing to work with young people and the young people we were ourselves once upon a time. There are easier and better-paid jobs to do, after all. There's more to it than needing to pay the rent. There's more to it than altruism. I think we do it for reasons which are more unconscious and personal than we'll admit, because working with young people inevitably affects our own remembered adolescence. This time around, we're the parent-figures. We can't help being reminded of those teenage years, re-connecting vicariously with whatever was wonderful or painful about that time and potentially amending, re-affirming or shedding fresh light on that experience. I remember a contented teacher once telling me that she'd had lots of jobs before becoming a teacher but teaching had finally 'fixed it' for her.

I wonder to myself how much Kamila unconsciously identifies herself with students needing love and support rather than with teachers sometimes obliged to make unpopular, punitive decisions. She may be enacting something unresolved in her relationship with her own parents whereby she can't bear to punish anyone because that identifies her with the two of them – harsh, unforgiving, ungenerous. Instead, she can only identify with her students – needy, misunderstood, unloved.

I ask what it would feel like to punish a student.

'Terrible!' she says. 'I'd probably cry and worry about it for days!'

'Because you'd feel like your parents?'

She looks bemused before starting to realise what I've suggested.

How can a parent-figure be firm and fond, clear and kind? Arguably, Kamila became a teacher in order to resolve that conflict. Yet every day it surfaces and remains unresolved. My guess is that until she can tell the difference between the harshness of her particular parents and the need for people in authority sometimes to be firm, she'll always struggle to be an effective teacher and the issue will affect all her relationships to a greater or lesser extent. Insisting on rules doesn't mean being unkind.

So with that conflict in mind, we'll talk about her parents, trying to understand why discipline came to be their only way of expressing love for their daughter. We'll think about all the things she felt like saying to them at the time but could never say for fear of reprisals. We'll grieve for the gentle, affectionate parents she needed as a young person but never really met. Once firmness and discipline are no longer separated from kindness and love in her mind, Kamila can become a good teacher. If she gives up teaching now, she'll only have to go elsewhere in her continuing attempt to resolve the issue.

I tell her this. She agrees. We start meeting regularly.

There are plenty of others... Greg feels bullied by the headteacher because of his students' poor exam results. Lucy is preoccupied with an ex-partner who keeps phoning at all hours. Ron thinks he's stagnating and wonders whether he should move to another school. Steve was involved in an upsetting incident with a student who took an overdose. Gail is so angry with the school that she doesn't want to go to her own leaving party. John wants to tell me why he should have been promoted. Julia is missing her partner and children who are living hundreds of miles away. Mina can't get pregnant. James is exhausted and sleeping badly...

Teachers are always dealing with loss. Working with children and young people every day, they're inevitably reminded of a childhood and adolescence now lost to them. They're reminded of lives they haven't led and lives they'll never lead now that they're older. 'Am I the same as other people or am I different?' Like young people and like parents, teachers worry about ordinariness as much as anyone, worrying whether they should be more of this or less of that. And as their students grow up and prepare to leave school, they're obliged to let go of young people in whom they've invested so much.

Some teachers are comfortable, or at least more *practised*, at dealing with this. Others aren't. It's hard not to have mixed feelings about students leaving for exciting futures full of financial, creative, sexual or hedonistic possibilities (Luxmoore 2008). There are strong feelings in the staffroom whenever a teacher announces that she's leaving to travel the world or go back to university or start a completely different job. 'What about me?' the others ask implicitly. '*What about me?*'

Nigel admits that, having lost his temper, he called one student a 'stupid bloody idiot' and the whole class 'a bunch of morons'. Inevitably, stories were told at home that evening and several parents duly complained the following morning. Nigel was summoned to see the headteacher who wanted to defend the actions of her staff but was concerned because this wasn't Nigel's first outburst and, at sixty-one years of age, having been a teacher for thirty-six years, he should have known better. She warned him of disciplinary measures against him should another of these incidents occur and advised him to talk to me.

He took her advice. 'I think I'm getting too old for this game,' he says, embarrassed, anxious about what I'll think. 'I've been at it for thirty-six years, ever since I left the army. Did you know that?'

I had no idea.

'A lot's changed in thirty-six years! Back in those days, students did as they were told. Teachers had respect. You put one foot out of place and that was that. Everyone knew where they stood.'

'You're right,' I say. 'A lot's changed.'

'Not all of it bad,' he adds, worrying in case I disapprove. 'Don't get me wrong – some things are better – but I came into teaching to help children learn and nowadays most of them aren't interested in that.'

I say nothing.

'You probably think I'm just old-fashioned but I remember the things we used to do back then... The trips we used to go on... I'll never forget those but, of course, you can't do anything like that nowadays because it's all health and safety and getting into trouble with the big boss if a child so much as sprains an ankle!'

Nigel has a reputation as a disciplinarian. I know this because I've heard about him from students, some of whom enjoy his straightforward authoritarianism but most of whom are scared and resentful of him. I know that he regularly shouts at classes and regularly gets away with it. I do disapprove but I also respect anyone who's been a teacher for thirty-six years because, in my experience, there's almost always something affectionate or idealistic hidden away behind even the most cynical or belligerent of teaching masks.

As with anyone, we go back to the beginning. His father left before Nigel can remember and Nigel was brought up by his mother. Joining the army made sense and he loved it – the camaraderie, the discipline ('knowing where you stood'), the sense of purpose.

He regales me with stories. I ask whether becoming a teacher was a way of offering young people something of what he'd enjoyed in the army.

He agrees. 'That's right! Most of them don't have what I had back in those days in the army and – I'm sorry but I have to say – I think they need it!'

I suggest that, in joining a staffroom, Nigel might have expected to find some of the things he'd enjoyed in the army.

Again he agrees and tells me fondly about members of staff from the old days, all now retired or dead.

I ask what it's like now, seeing the young teachers arrive, full of energy and ambition, wanting to make a difference.

'Takes me back!' he jokes. 'I see myself in them sometimes.'

We pause.

I ask what that feels like.

His eyes are glistening and he's aware that I've noticed. 'There you are! You've got me, haven't you! Got me on a weak spot! I suppose that's why you're the counsellor!'

I ask again what it feels like, seeing these young teachers arrive.

'Yeah…' he says, swallowing and trying to recover his composure, '…sad. It *is* sad, I won't pretend. I'm not getting any younger and I'm not going anywhere in teaching now, am I! I'm building up to retirement and then that'll be me done. Thank you very much. Clock on the mantelpiece and off you go!'

His sense of being discarded as a teacher (possibly going all the way back to feeling discarded by his father) makes Nigel angry and makes him sad. He's angry in the classroom and sad with me. We talk about his original idealism as a teacher, wanting students to enjoy what he'd enjoyed in the army (and not feel discarded). We talk about how hard it is nowadays to hold on to that idealism while the system keeps changing, while younger teachers get promoted and sixty-one-year-old teachers become has-beens, taken for granted by their colleagues and by students. The frustration erupts in his classroom outbursts.

He agrees. (Like a son, anxious for my approval, he tends to agree with me.)

I ask what he imagines retirement will be like.

Suddenly he comes to life. 'That won't be a problem! I've got more than enough to do!' He tells me about his allotment – the vegetables, the flowers, the people he knows, the seasonal shifts and how they affect the soil. He smiles, pleased that I'm interested.

'I never knew any of this, Nigel!'

'Most people don't. I suppose I keep it to myself. But it's what I enjoy doing.'

I want to say something clever about tending a garden and tending a child. But don't.

Afterword

I'd just finished the first draft of this book when I was invited to speak at the AGM of a local counselling organisation. Good, I thought – a chance to try out some of these ideas. I'll talk about the curse of ordinariness and see what they think.

Usually I'm a confident speaker. I can be funny and fluent and I'm able to explain ideas clearly. But on this occasion it was different. As I started to talk, I got nervous and for some reason my nerves wouldn't go away. I drank water and tried to relax, but it made no difference: my mouth stayed dry, my breathing shallow and I knew I was rushing everything. I apologised and carried on, hoping that my nerves would go away. But they didn't. Only during the questions at the end did I improve.

Maybe I was still too close to the book. Maybe I felt unsure of my ground because I hadn't talked about ordinariness in public before. Maybe I was trying to cram in too much material or maybe, for some other reason, I was just spooked by the occasion.

A friend was in the audience. He came over as the meeting broke up and as people were beginning to chat to each other over coffee.

I apologised all over again for being so nervous.

'No, it was fine,' he said. 'The best thing about it was your ordinariness!'

I thought about this, driving home, embarrassed and – like all the people in this book – not at all sure how I felt about being ordinary.

References

Arnold, M. (1879) (ed.) 'Ode on Imitations of Mortality.' In *Poems of Wordsworth*. London: Macmillan.

Balindt, M. (1968) *The Basic Fault*. Evanston, IL: Northwestern University Press.

Bateson, G. (1979) *Mind and Nature: A Necessary Unity*. New York, NY: Bantam Books.

Bennett, A. (2005) *Untold Stories*. London: Faber.

Bettelheim, B. (1976) *The Uses of Enchantment*. London: Thames and Hudson.

Blomkvist, L.D. and Rutzel, T. (1994) 'Surplus Reality and Beyond.' In P. Holmes, M. Karp and M. Watson (eds) *Psychodrama Since Moreno*. London: Routledge.

Blos, P. (1962) *On Adolescence: A Psychoanalytic Interpretation*. New York, NY: The Free Press.

Bollas, C. (1987) *The Shadow of the Object*. London: Free Association Books.

Brooks, L. (2009) 'The Susan Boyle myth.' *The Guardian*, 28 May 2009.

Caldwell, P. (2007) *From Isolation to Intimacy*. London: Jessica Kingsley Publishers.

Coren, A. (1997) *A Psychodynamic Approach to Education*. London: Sheldon Press.

Cullen, D. (2009) *Columbine*. London: Old Street Publishing.

Dewey, J. (1934) *A Common Faith*. New Haven, CT: Yale University Press.

Ehrenreich, B. (2009) *Smile or Die: How Positive Thinking Fooled America and the World*. London: Granta Publications.

Freud, S. (1912) *Totem and Taboo*. London: Hogarth Press.

Freud, S. (1914) *On Narcissism*. London: Hogarth Press.

Freud, S. (1930) *Civilisation and Its Discontents*. London: Hogarth Press.

Freud, S. (2001) 'Formulations of the Two Principles of Mental Functioning.' In *The Complete Psychological Works of Sigmund Freud: Vol. 12*. London: Vintage. (Original work published 1911.)

Freud, S. (2001) 'The Unconscious.' In *The Complete Psychological Works of Sigmund Freud: Vol. 14*. London: Vintage. (Original work published 1915.)

Freud, S. (2001) 'Group Psychology and the Analysis of the Ego.' In *The Complete Psychological Works of Sigmund Freud: Vol. 18*. London: Vintage. (Original work published 1921.)

Freud, S. (2001) 'The Future of an Illusion.' In *The Complete Psychological Works of Sigmund Freud: Vol. 21*. London: Vintage. (Original work published 1927.)

Frost, R. (2001) 'The Road Not Taken.' In E.C. Lathem (ed.) *The Poetry of Robert Frost*. London: Jonathan Cape. (Original work published 1920.)

Gladwell, M. (2008) *Outliers*. London: Penguin Books.

Guntrip, H. (1968) *Schizoid Phenomena, Object Relations and the Self*. London: Hogarth Press.

Hodgson Burnett, F. (1987) *The Secret Garden*. Oxford: Oxford University Press. (Original work published 1911.)

Howitt, P. (1998) *Sliding Doors*. USA: Miramax Films.

Jacobs, M. (1985) *The Presenting Past*. Buckingham: Open University Press.

James, W. (1985) *The Varieties of Religious Experience*. London: Penguin Books. (Original work published 1902.)

Jung, C.G. (1933) *Modern Man in Search of a Soul*. London: Kegan Paul.

Jung, C.G. (1972) *Four Archetypes*. London: Routledge & Kegan Paul Ltd.

Kafka, F. (1961) *Metamorphosis and Other Stories*. London: Penguin Modern Classics. (Original work published 1916.)

Kahr, B. (2007) *Sex and the Psyche*. London: Penguin Books.

Klein, M. (1946) 'Notes on Some Schizoid Mechanisms.' In M. Klein, P. Heimann, S. Isaacs and J. Riviere (eds) *Developments in Psychoanalysis*. London: Hogarth Press.

Klein, M. (1957) *Envy and Gratitude: A Study of Unconscious Sources*. London: Tavistock Publications.

Kohut, H. (1971) *The Analysis of the Self: A Systematic Approach to the Treatment of Narcissistic Personality Disorders*. New York, NY: International Universities Press.

Larkin, P. (1955) 'Born Yesterday' from *The Less Deceived*. London: Faber.

Levens, M. (1995) *Eating Disorders and Magical Control of the Body*. London: Routledge.

Lomas, P. (1973) *True and False Experience*. New Brunswick: Transaction Publishers.

Luxmoore, N. (2000) *Listening to Young People in School, Youth Work and Counselling*. London: Jessica Kingsley Publishers.

Luxmoore, N. (2006) *Working with Anger and Young People*. London: Jessica Kingsley Publishers.

Luxmoore, N. (2008) *Feeling like Crap: Young People and the Meaning of Self-Esteem.* London: Jessica Kingsley Publishers.

Luxmoore, N. (2010) *Young People in Love and in Hate.* London: Jessica Kingsley Publishers.

MacNeice, L. (1964) 'Selva Oscura' from *Selected Poems of Louis MacNeice.* London: Faber & Faber.

Marineau, R.F. (1989) *Jacob Levy Moreno 1889–1974.* London: Tavistock/Routledge.

Meltzer, D. and Harris Williams, M. (1988) *The Apprehension of Beauty: The Role of Aesthetic Conflict in Development, Art and Violence.* Perthshire: Clunie Press.

Newsome, D.H. (1974) *Two Classes of Men: Platonism and English Romantic Thought.* London: John Murray Publishers.

Nussbaum, M.C. (2001) *Upheavals of Thought.* Cambridge: Cambridge University Press.

Papadopoulos, R.K. (2002) 'Refugees, Home and Trauma.' In R.K. Papadopoulos (ed.) *Therapeutic Care for Refugees.* London: Karnac Books.

Phillips, A. (1993) *On Kissing, Tickling and Being Bored.* London: Faber.

Phillips, A. (1998) *The Beast in the Nursery.* London: Faber.

Rogers, C. (1961) *On Becoming a Person.* Boston, MA: Houghton Mifflin.

Schreurs, A. (2002) *Psychotherapy and Spirituality.* London: Jessica Kingsley Publishers.

Schwartz, D. (2003) 'In Dreams Begin Responsibilities.' In *In Dreams Begin Responsibilities and Other Stories.* London: Souvenir Press. (Original work published 1948.)

Shaffer, P. (1980) *Amadeus.* London: Penguin Books.

Williamson, M. (1992) *A Return to Love: Reflections on the Principles of a Course in Miracles.* New York, NY: HarperCollins.

Winnicott, D.W. (1965) *The Maturational Processes and the Facilitating Environment.* London: Hogarth Press.

Winnicott, D.W. (1971) *Playing and Reality.* London: Routledge.

Winnicott, D.W. (1975) *Through Paediatrics to Psycho-Analysis.* London: Hogarth Press.

Wolf, E.S. (1980) 'Developmental Line of Self–Object Relations.' In A. Goldberg (ed.) *Advances in Self Psychology.* New York, NY: International Universities Press.

Wood, J.V., Perunovic, W.Q.E. and Lee, J.W. (2009) 'Positive self-statements: Power for some, peril for others.' *Psychological Science 20*, 860–866.

Yalom, I.D. (2008) *Staring at the Sun: Overcoming the Dread of Death.* London: Piatkus Books.

Index